LIBRARY IN A BOOK

EATING DISORDERS

THE FACTS ON FILE LIBRARY IN A BOOK SERIES

Each volume of the Facts On File Library in a Book series is carefully designed to be the best one-volume source for research on important current problems. Written clearly and carefully so that even the most complex aspects of the issue are easily understandable, the books give the reader the research tools to begin work, plus the information needed to delve more deeply into the topic. Each book includes a history of the subject, biographical information on important figures in the field, a complete annotated bibliography and a carefully designed index—everything the researcher needs to get down to work.

LIBRARY IN A BOOK

EATING DISORDERS

John R. Matthews

Facts On File

New York • Oxford

LIBRARY IN A BOOK: EATING DISORDERS

Copyright © 1991 by John R. Matthews

All rights reserved. No part of this book may be reproduced or utilized in any form or by any means, electronic or mechanical, including photocopying, recording, or by any information storage or retrieval systems, without permission in writing from the publisher. For information contact:

Facts On File, Inc.	Facts On File Limited
460 Park Avenue South	Collins Street
New York NY 10016	Oxford OX4 1XJ
USA	United Kingdom

Library of Congress Cataloging-in-Publication Data
Matthews, John R.
    Library in a book: eating disorders / John R. Matthews.
        p.   cm.
    Includes bibliographical references and index.
    ISBN 0–8160–1911–8
    1. Eating disorders.   I. Title
    RC552.E18M38
    616.85′26 — dc20   90–40323

A British CIP catalogue record for this book is available from the British Library.

Facts On File books are available at special discounts when purchased in bulk quantities for businesses, associations, institutions or sales promotions. Please call our Special Sales Department in New York at 212/683-2244 (dial 800/322-8755 except in NY, AK or HI) or in Oxford at 865/728399.

ISBN 0-8160-1911-8

Series text design by Ron Monteleone
Jacket design by Nadja Furlan–Lorbek
Composition by the Maple-Vail Book Manufacturing Group
Manufactured by the Maple-Vail Book Manufacturing Group
Printed in the United States of America

10 9 8 7 6 5 4 3 2 1

This book is printed on acid-free paper.

CONTENTS

PART I
EATING DISORDERS   1

Chapter 1
History and Treatment   3
Obesity   5
Anorexia Nervosa   29
Bulimia   39
Other Eating Disorders   48
Trends for the Future   48

Chapter 2
Chronology   51

Chapter 3
Legal Issues Relating to Eating Disorders   75

Chapter 4
Biographies   81

PART II
GUIDE TO FURTHER RESEARCH   89

Glossary   91

Acronyms and Initials   97

Government Programs   99

Organizations   101

Libraries and Special Collections   105

v

Contents

Special Programs for Schools and Organizations 107

Bibliography 109

Appendix 151

Index 157

LIBRARY IN A BOOK

EATING DISORDERS

PART I

EATING DISORDERS

CHAPTER 1

HISTORY AND TREATMENT

The subject of eating disorders has evolved into distinct medical and psychological categories only during the last few years, and the resulting study and treatment has opened important pathways of help for sufferers. Most major medical schools and teaching hospitals now have eating disorders clinics, and more practitioners in various medical and psychological disciplines are devoting their careers to study and treatment of the problem.

Unlike many psychological disorders and addictions that pose little physical threat to their victims, eating disorder patients may suffer grave physical health threats; indeed, many anorectics are near death by the time treatment begins. For this reason, greater public awareness of the symptoms and consequences of disordered eating is important. The sooner parents, doctors and others recognize the early warning symptoms of disordered eating, the greater the prospect for successful treatment.

Anorexia nervosa has been called a "disease of abundance." It is not known anywhere except in the affluent parts of the world, where food is plentiful and cheap. Although it was first named in the 19th century and has been known and described throughout history, anorexia is considered a fairly recent phenomenon because its incidence appears to be increasing. Certainly the awareness of its incidence is increasing due to the growing interest of medical professionals in its treatment.

Bulimia has only recently been recognized and named, gaining increased attention during the 1980s. It was briefly thought to be epidemic among college students, but recent studies reveal that the initial fears about its incidence have been exaggerated. Still, relatively little is known about the disorder and its relationship to other psychological distur-

3

bances. Until recently, bulimia was a "secret disorder," with each sufferer supposing herself to be its only victim. As more victims emerge seeking treatment, more attention will be focused on the need for greater research and study, increasing the prospects for successful treatment.

The categorizing of obesity itself as an eating disorder is somewhat an anomaly; obesity is really more of a symptom than a disorder—much as emaciation is a symptom of anorexia nervosa. And in the same way that emaciation may be a symptom of something other than an eating disorder—tuberculosis or AIDS, for example—obesity may also be symptomatic of conditions other than disordered eating. Many specialists do not regard obesity caused by metabolic malfunctions as an eating disorder per se and question whether or not it should be included in the literature of eating disorders.

Kelly Brownell and John Forety, the editors of the *Eating Disorders Handbook*, while recognizing the anomaly, argue that obesity should be regarded as a disorder in itself because obesity research is so closely related to other aspects of eating disorders, and they point out that advances in one area will impact all other areas if considered together as one discipline. For that reason in our overview on obesity we have shown the condition in all its aspects, even its contributions to the causes of diabetes. One of the major difficulties in the management of obesity has been the tendency of those treating it to regard it as simply a problem of overeating, whereas it may be caused by one of many factors. Consequently the obese person with a metabolic disorder may have been treated very similarly to the obese person who compulsively overeats—very much like treating an anorectic patient for tuberculosis. This one-treatment–fits–all approach is probably responsible for the very low success rate and the very high frustration rate for the treatment failure of overweight conditions. However, many health practitioners, especially those who are themselves recovering from eating disorders, are suspicious of widespread claims of obesity caused by anything other than overeating. They point out that the overeater, like the alcoholic, is often in a state of denial, failing to recognize his own overeating, and assigning the cause to slowed metabolism or genetic dysfunction.

As scientific knowledge about eating disorders advances, the eating disordered individual is more and more being seen as a component in a disordered system, and newer forms of therapy are beginning to address those systems failures. In many cases these therapies are finding gratifying responses, giving hope to individuals with eating disorders.

OBESITY

INTRODUCTION

In some respects obesity is the easiest of eating disorders to understand, its clinical definition the simplest, its physiological causes—an imbalance of energy intake and output—rooted in the most elemental biology. At its extreme, obesity is obviously a serious disorder and as such has been in the medical lexicon for a very long time. Yet the study of obesity beyond those most basic elements provokes wide disagreement, partly because of this simplicity. Because its physiology is so simple, the prescription for its cure is also both simple and logical: reduce energy intake to reverse the direction of the energy imbalance. However, obesity has not yielded to conventional wisdom and logic, and the obese have remained obese, leaving doctors frustrated and even angry, and leaving the obese bewildered, with feelings of failure, guilt and worthlessness. The major problem with obesity management has not been weight loss, which is relatively easy; it has been with maintenance of weight, which thus far has eluded widespread success.

Researchers have been fascinated with the failure of the simplistic models of obesity management and have developed numerous theories to account for obesity's persistence. The biological and physical aspects have long been understood, and progress in confirming some of the more astute intuitions about genetic aspects has been made just in the last year or two; the psychological aspects of obesity are more elusive.

Researchers have themselves at times been frustrated; they need to be well grounded in two disparate realms of science: biology and psychology, each with unique study methods, not easily meshed. Moreover, the psychological and social aspects of obesity are difficult to factor into broad scale surveys on the physical aspects and yet are essential to bring scientific order to the subject.

Many older studies have had to rely on mercurial statistics, gathered through a multiplicity of agencies such as insurance industry and government health agencies, many using no uniform standards of measure, and many of which studied unrepresentative populations or otherwise distorted demographics, Physical surveys and studies of special populations abound, and we have cited some of them throughout the text.

Some order has begun to emerge from the chaos that is obesity study, some common sense confirmed, some theories discarded, Yet, some myths and prejudices remain.

DEFINING OBESITY

Fat, the ostensible villain of obesity, is an essential element in the makeup of the human body. Most body fat is stored in the subcutaneous layer—the layer just below the epidermis, the body's outer covering. The body uses fat in many ways. It has a cushioning effect: Fatter people are less readily injured by shock or trauma. It insulates the body against excessive swings in temperature. It has cosmetic uses in smoothing the skin: Skin without a subcutaneous fat layer would be flabby and wrinkled. Most important, it is stored energy for times when the body may be deprived of food for long periods, such as during famines or lengthy debilitating illnesses.

The body is an efficient manufacturer of fat. Regardless of its chemical composition, all food that is not utilized in tissue replacement nor burned as energy is converted to fat and stored in various places in the body. Over long periods, if the body's energy intake is greater than its energy output, the result is overweight or obesity.

Briefly then, obesity is an excess of body fat above the norm. Obesity is generally measured in highly subjective gradations such as overweight, moderately obese and massively or morbidly obese. It is important to distinguish between being merely overweight and being obese. Some overweight people—some athletes for example—are not obese at all, and some people who do not appear to be overweight may in fact be obese.

The reasons some people are heavier than others are many, varied, complex and—except for obesity caused by overeating—not well understood. It is generally agreed that obesity begins when one weighs about 20% above the norm.

MEASURING WEIGHT NORMS
Ideal Weights

The definition of what weight ranges constitute ideals is somewhat confusing. Health professionals argue convincingly that weight ranges appearing to be associated with the greatest longevity are the only sensible measure of the ideal. In theory most would agree; however, there has been wide disagreement about how to measure optimum weights objectively, and consequently there has been some confusion and inconsistency in the study of all aspects of nutrition and eating disorders.

Height and Weight Charts

Height and weight charts have been around in one form or another since 1912. The charts themselves, which are based on insurance industry actuarial figures, give a range of ideal weights for various heights, and the weight ranges for some heights can vary more than 20 pounds, particularly within the large–frame category, leaving a huge gap of imprecision. Twenty pounds is 13.5% of the weight of a person weighing 150 pounds, and 20% above ideal is considered the threshold of obesity.

The height and weight chart used as the standard is the Metropolitan Height and Weight Tables, first published in 1959 and revised and reissued in 1983. The new tables give ideal weights and heights quite different from those in the earlier chart. Both are based on actuarial longevity figures compiled by the insurance industry, and there is no indication why ideal weights should have changed in such a brief span as 24 years. Ideal weights in the 1983 chart are as much as 18 pounds heavier for men and 13 pounds heavier for women than those of the 1959 chart, particularly at the shorter–stature end of the chart.

The Metropolitan Life Insurance Company has no explanation for the heavier weights in the 1983 chart. In July 1988 *The New York Times* quoted Dr. Charles B. Arnold, a medical director at Metropolitan as saying, "We don't even like to use the term 'ideal weight' or 'desirable weight' anymore. There are too many interpretations that might be applied. We weren't saying it was all right to be heavier [referring to the weight differences in the two charts]. All we were saying was that heavy people seemed to have a lower mortality in 1983 than in 1959 based on study of life insurance policy holders."

The Metropolitan Height and Weight Tables give ideal weight ranges for three categories at each height: small frame, medium frame and large frame. At each height the weight range difference from the lowest in the small frame category to the heaviest in the large frame category might be as much as 41 pounds, so it is very important for users of the tables to first determine frame size.

To measure frame size the Metropolitan has devised an "elbow measure" in which the distance in inches is measured between the two knobby bones on either side of the elbow, using a caliper. The elbow chart (see Appendix) then gives frame sizes based on height and elbow measure.

Because the charts are based on data gathered at the time individuals buy insurance there is no way of statistically comparing any changes that occur after that. Insurance companies do not gather height and weight data at an individual's death, and death certificates do not list it.

Critics of these tables point out that the insurance policy purchasers from whom these statistics were compiled were disproportionately male, white and upper income, and therefore not representative of the population as a whole. Dr. Reubin Andres, a federal researcher, has recently completed a new analysis of the actuarial data used to produce the tables and has concluded that the tables' weight ranges are too high for young people, about right for people in their early 40s and too low for middle–aged and older people. He also concluded that there should be no differences by sex in ideal weight ranges.

Despite complaints about the charts, nutritionists regard them as the best available measure. In addition, since the charts are so widely used, they at least provide some consistency in discussions of weight problems and provide a uniform standard in defining who is and is not overweight and obese.

Other Measures of Ideal Weights

One rule of thumb some doctors use to determine ideal weight is called the "magic 36," which says that if waist circumference in inches subtracted from height in inches is less than 36, one is probably overweight.

Another general rule states that at a height of 60 inches, women should ideally weigh 100 pounds and men should weigh 105 pounds, and for every inch above 60, the weight for women should increase by five pounds and for men, six pounds.

Other tests include the "belt" test, in which one is considered overweight if the circumference of the chest at the nipples is smaller than the waist measurement; the "pinch test," in which folds at various parts of the body are measured; and various chemical and physical measurements using instruments such as the densimeter and the hydrometer, which measure specific gravity (the weight to volume ratio of a solid or liquid compared to a weight/volume standard such as water). Specific gravity of fat body mass and lean tissue differ, so these instruments can determine the ratio of fat to lean muscle tissue.

Some sports doctors, who are accustomed to treating patients in top physical condition, use a measure that indicates ideal weights are much lower than those advocated by other health professionals. To determine ideal weight for a male, they multiply his height in inches by four. Then subtract 128 to get the ideal weight in pounds. For women, they multiply height by three and one–half and subtract 108. They then make adjustments up or down for frame size.

Of the ones mentioned, the two most commonly used obesity measures are the height/weight tables and the skinfold "pinch" test. Doctors Carl Seltzer, of the Harvard University School of Public Health, and Jean Mayer, now president of Tufts University, both in Boston, prefer the skinfold test, pointing out that *obesity* and *overweight* are not necessarily equivalent and that the important measure is that of proportion of fat, which can be more accurately measured with the skinfold test. For example, many young football athletes are overweight but not obese—

not having a large proportion of fat to muscle—and some extremely sedentary people may have normal weights according to their heights but still be obese, having a large proportion of fat to muscle.

Perhaps the most common diagnostic method is simply visual observation. Certainly most doctors, and most laymen as well, have pre–formed opinions about what an obese person looks like and whether he is massively obese, moderately obese or simply slightly overweight. The tests are then used to provide more precision and confirm the visual diagnosis.

Health and Weight Surveys

The U.S. Health Service has produced studies of average or median weights for different age groups and various other age–weight statistics, but these studies have no direct relation to the various ideal weight measures. The U.S. Public Health Service has also undertaken a random national survey which measured maximum average weights of men and women using age and height as variables. This survey found, among other things, that as men and women aged, women became heavier than men relative to their early–year weights. However, since women statistically outlive men, the survey findings would tend to suggest that later–life weight gains are both normal and healthy. However, both men and women are living longer for a variety of reasons: development of drugs and other disease treatments, better preventive health care and better nutrition.

At the same time, both men and women have become more sedentary. Whereas once more than half the U.S. working population worked at manual labor, today even manual jobs no longer require great expenditures of energy: Forklifts do all the heavy lifting, harvest machinery is almost entirely automatic and few people walk any greater distance than from parking lot to car. Some people have combated this growing sedentary movement with physical exercise, but by no means the majority.

Health professionals hypothesize that this sedentary life style is at least partially responsible for the greater recent weight norms. It is also possible that better nutrition is partially responsible. It was once thought that better nutrition and more plentiful food was largely responsible for the greater growth in height in children of immigrant groups, but it is now generally agreed that the more likely reason is the crossbreeding that has occurred as immigrant groups settled throughout the country.

WHO ARE THE OBESE?

Obesity in the U.S. is class related, and it is more prevalent at the low end of the economic scale than at the high end. The reasons for this are not fully understood, but health professionals suspect that it is a product of social values: Obesity, and even moderate overweight, are taboo among the rich, but less so among the working class. In addition working–class people may lack the resources for expensive weight reduction treatments and high–energy activities that help keep weight down. There may also be some genetic tendencies to obesity in some ethnic groups. It is known that some, Eskimos for example, tend to have slower metabolisms and are more prone to being overweight.

Obesity prevalence is also sex related. The Health and Nutrition Examination Survey of the National Center for Health Statistics (NCHS) shows that 12% of men and 23% of women aged 20 to 74 are obese. Age is also a factor. Both men and women tend to add weight as they age. Because body weight tends to increase with age, some researchers are even suggesting that the increased body weight contributes to longevity. It is true that although women tend to become heavier relative to their mean weights at an earlier age than men, women have a greater life expectancy.

Obesity is difficult to measure in children because children's growth patterns are erratic and some seemingly obese children develop into normal weight adults. However, it has been found that most obese adults were obese as children.

Perceptions of overweight are more prevalent than the actual incidence of overweight, and twice as many people in the NCHS survey rated themselves as overweight as actually were. In the same survey, 64% of those who rated themselves as overweight were trying to lose weight.

An article in *Glamour* in 1984 analyzed a survey the magazine had conducted earlier. The survey revealed that 75% of the respondents "felt too fat," although the survey data indicated that only 25% of the respondents were overweight. It further found that 45% of respondents who were actually underweight felt they were too fat, and 66% of those want to diet because they feel too fat. The survey percentages do not have any validity in measuring the population as a whole. The survey questionnaire was published in the magazine and readers were asked to respond, therefore the respondents were self–selecting and did not represent a random sampling of the magazine's readers. The survey results are further distorted by the demographic profile of the magazine's readers, which, according to *Standard Rate and Data Service*, are "working women between the ages of 18 and 34." However, even considering these distortions of the data, the number of people, especially women, who consider themselves overweight even though they are underweight or at least normal weight, is revealing of the dimensions of the confusion about overweight and obesity.

CAUSES OF OBESITY

Scientists have speculated that humans' ability to store fat is a survival adaptation from prehistoric eras before mankind learned to grow and store food. Hunter–gatherers did not eat three well regulated meals per day, but ate whenever food was available; thus, the ability to store energy in the form of fat allowed people to go days or weeks without eating, and yet suffer no ill effects. Even some modern primitive people, such as Eskimos, are adapted to a feast and famine syndrome. Studies have shown that Eskimos have a much more efficient metabolism than other people; that is, their bodies are able to produce a greater amount of work with a lesser degree of energy expenditure.

Perhaps one of the fiercest and least conclusive debates in medical history has been about the causes of obesity, with one school of thought—once prevalent—holding that all obese people are fat because they eat excessive amounts of food. The other school of thought—now gaining ground—holds that much obesity, perhaps even most, is caused by genetic factors. The truth is beginning to emerge somewhere in the middle, with both schools of thought being right part of the time; obesity appears now to have multiple causes both in the obese population as a whole as well as within some individual cases.

Judith Rodin, a researcher, writing in *Psychological Aspects of Obesity*, Benjamin B. Wolman, ed., has expressed the frustration scientists feel regarding obesity and its causes:

> *The causes of obesity may be multifactorial. Its onset is determined by a combination of genetic, psychological, and environmental factors, and thus far it has been difficult to disentangle the relative importance of each component. Perhaps this is the reason that for us as scientists, as well as for the overweight person, dealing with obesity sometimes feels like such a losing battle.*

Many diagnosticians give a quick and curt answer to the question of what causes obesity: overeating. Unfortunately, like other simplistic views of the problem, this response fails to differentiate between the psychological aspects of excessive and binge eating as an eating disorder and the biological aspects of obesity, which may be beyond the individual's control. However, technically the insensitive diagnostician is correct: For purposes of definition, overeaters are simply people who have a larger food intake than is normal for people for their height and build, regardless of metabolism or genetic factors.

Genetic Factors

For years some obese people have complained, "I hardly eat anything, and yet I gain weight." Doctors often countered with, "If you could follow fat people for 24 hours per day, writing down everything they ate, you would find at the end of the day that they had consumed vast amounts of food." In fact one diet strategy of many doctors was to have obese patients make a note every time they put something into their mouths, noting what it was, how much and the time it was consumed. When patients returned with lists indicating they ate no more than a normal amount of food, some doctors accused them of cheating, or perhaps of even eating unconsciously, forgetting to make a note. It now appears that these doctors may have been unfair to many of their patients. Two studies published in the *New England Journal of Medicine* in 1988 have established that slowed metabolism may play an important role in obesity.

One study focused on Pima Indians in Arizona, who are prone to obesity, and measured their metabolism at rest. The study followed one group two years and found that those who gained the most weight burned 80 fewer calories per day than was normal for their body sizes. The researchers calculated that at that rate, subjects would gain nine pounds per year. They followed another group for four years and concluded that those with the lowest metabolism rates were the likeliest to become overweight. They found similar metabolic rates within family groups, indicating that the tendency to obesity is inherited. This study made no attempt to determine which, if any, subjects ate more than the nonobese.

The other study reported by the *New England Journal of Medicine* looked at infants in England, considering babies born to both thin and overweight women. Researchers measured their metabolic rates at age three months and found that about half the babies born to overweight mothers burned about 21% fewer calories than the other babies and were overweight by the time they were one year old. The other babies' weights were normal. The obese babies ate no more than those of normal weight.

Dr. Jules Hirsch of Rockefeller University, in New York City, has found that obese people tend to have normal rates of metabolism when they are fat, but when they lose weight, their metabolic rate goes down, making it extremely difficult to stay thin. In an editorial in the *New England Journal of Medicine*, Dr. Hirsch commented on one of the perplexities of body weight:

> *Most people, whether lean or obese, tend to remain at the same weight for long periods. This means that the change in their body's stored energy is usually zero, and therefore the energy content of the food they ingest is in balance with their energy expenditure. This fact is in itself remarkable. Small, persistent deviations from balance would lead to large increases or decreases in fat storage. Most of us are unaware of controlling caloric intake or physical activity to the level of precision required to keep energy stores constant for many years.*

History and Treatment

In the same editorial Hirsch has also written:

> . . . *it is often assumed that obesity is a disorder of food intake, pure and simple, and that energy expenditure does not play much of a part in determining energy balance.*
> . . . *Persons who were formerly obese often have a lower caloric requirement for weight maintenance than those who have never been obese. Their expenditure and intake of energy are equal, but are at lower levels than those in persons who have never been obese.*
> . . . *thermogenesis has been shown . . . to be important in the development, though not the maintenance, of obesity.*

For reasons that are at least partially explained by Dr. Hirsch's comment, some experts are saying that dieting itself can be a cause of obesity. Long before these studies were published in the *New England Journal of Medicine*, Sharon Greene Patton in her book, *Stop Dieting—Start Living*, made a passionate argument for dieting as a cause of obesity because of genetic factors:

> *The more you diet, the more efficient your body becomes at conserving calories, until finally it can become impossible for you to lose weight even on a starvation diet.*
> *Scientists think this is similar to hibernation. Animals' metabolisms slow down to nearly zero so that they can live off their reserves while sleeping through the winter. What causes this response is still a mystery; however, researchers have found that humans react in the same way during starvation: "Researchers have shown in their work with human subjects vastly lowered metabolic rates are normal responses to prolonged starvation—presumably because lowering metabolism lets the animal eke out existing glucose supplies for use by the brain for the longest possible amount of time." [Anne Scott Beller*, Fat and Thin: A Natural History of Obesity. New York: Farrar, Straus and Giroux, 1977.] The body reacts to reduced food intake by slowing down the metabolic rate, thus making it even more difficult to lose weight.*

Obesity as a contributor to diabetes has long been known; however, it is less well known that diabetes, specifically obese maturity–onset diabetes, itself is a cause of obesity, particularly in the way the body uses and produces insulin. In addition it has been shown that the obese are more hyperinsulinemic than normal weight people. Hyperinsulinemia (elevated basal insulin levels) affects the obese in direct relation to their degree of overweight—the more obese, the higher the insulin levels. It is believed that hyperinsulinemia enhances fat storage by accelerating the rate at which glucose, the end metabolic product of all ingested nutrients, is metabolized by adipose cells, thus producing more fat. Glucose in turn is a factor in the level of insulin released, which continues the vicious cycle of more insulin and more glucose conversion to fat. Hyperinsulinemia appears also to increase hunger.

A study of male twins published in 1986 in the *Journal of the American Medical Association* indicates that most obesity is an inherited tendency. Another study, by Dr. Albert Stunkard of the University of Pennsylvania School of Medicine in Philadelphia, indicates that adopted children more often develop weights consistent with biological rather than adoptive parents, another strong indication that the tendency to obesity is inherited.

Overeating is probably a factor in at least some instances in which obesity is primarily caused by slowed metabolism; however because overeating is a difficult variable to measure in large and prolonged studies such as those undertaken to demonstrate metabolic causes, there is no way of knowing how widespread it is in that population. Since any food intake above what the body needs for energy is overeating, persons with slowed metabolism could be described as people with lower food needs, and therefore food amounts that would be normal for others would be overeating for them.

Psychological Factors

Despite the excitement about the confirmation of slowed metabolism as a cause of obesity, the psychological and emotional factors long blamed for overweight will not go away. It has been well documented that at least some overeating is a response to factors such as stress and anxiety. It is not known if these responses have any genetic causes. Studies have demonstrated that obese subjects respond to anxiety and other emotional forms of stress by eating. Normal subjects do not.

One study showed that nearly 30% of obese people surveyed responded to emotional arousal by eating, whereas only 8% of nonobese subjects responded by eating. The obese subjects ate in response to feelings of social isolation, loneliness or depression.

In another study a cross section of patients seeking therapy for depression or anxiety or both were surveyed. More than half of the obese patients lost weight, while some gained and others remained the same. There was little weight change in the nonobese. Unfortunately it is not known if the weight losses were permanent or short–lived, an important omission that would color any conclusions to be drawn from the study.

Dr. Marcia Millman, in her book, *Such a Pretty Face*, tells of obese women's responses to the social pressures and their relationships with food. Time after time in interviews women described their overeating habits as being responsive to feelings of rejection because of their obesity, as comforter in times of loneliness and as tranquilizer. Some described bingeing and compulsive eating. One woman told of eating cookies her child had prepared for her grandmother, about the shame she felt about her inability to refrain from eating the cookies.

It is possible that the emotional problems described and studied by the experts were the result of the obesity rather than the cause of it. Many experts contend that studies of obese subjects find them no more nor less disturbed than a similar cross section of a nonobese population, and it should be emphasized that the studies showing the obese subjects' eating response to emotional pressure did not reveal the obese as being more or less psychologically maladjusted than the nonobese. After all, the nonobese also have feelings of rejection, loneliness and isolation, but they are less likely to respond by overeating.

Like many other treatment professionals, Tennie McCarty, director of Shades of Hope treatment center in Buffalo Gap, Texas is skeptical of research statistics that rely on questionnaire information to support non-eating causes of obesity. While not disputing the wide range of possible metabolic and genetic factors in producing heavier or lighter body types, once one's weight has gone beyond these slight variables into massive obesity, she regards it very likely—almost to a certainty—that the obesity is caused by overeating.

Herself a recovering overeater, McCarty is very frank about the compulsive overeater's state of denial. "We lie a lot about our eating," she says. "We lie to our doctors, our friends and families—and certainly we lie to questionnaires. And of course we lie to ourselves. Many compulsive overeaters are able to convince themselves that their food intake is normal."

Decreased Physical Activity

Another factor in causing and maintaining obesity is inactivity. Metabolism is probably influenced by exercise; certainly fewer calories are burned in a state of inactivity. One study used pedometers to measure distances walked by normal and obese individuals having the same age and similar occupations. The obese individuals walked significantly less than the others.

A clear demonstration of inactivity as a cause of overweight is military basic training. Recruits lined up at the beginning of "boot camp" represent a fair cross section of physical specimens in the 17 to 20 age group and include the underweight as well as overweight and sedentary. After a six- to eight-week program of rigorous exercise, it is found that the underweight recruits have gained and most of the overweight have lost weight. It is significant that there are few restrictions on food intake; most weight loss during the period is a result of physical exercise.

Researchers have also found that for some people fidgeting may be an important way to burn calories; restless people may squirm and wiggle away as many calories every day as several miles of jogging.

MEDICAL ASPECTS OF OBESITY

The Role of Obesity in Disease

It has long been known that obesity is a contributing factor to many diseases and disorders, particularly diabetes and hypertension. It is also known that the obese suffer about one and one–half times more heart attacks than the nonobese. Obesity is also a contributing factor in many other disorders: arteriosclerosis, angina pectoris, varicose veins, cirrhosis of the liver and kidney disease.

Obesity and obese maturity–onset diabetes have a pathologic symbiotic relationship. In most cases of juvenile–onset diabetes, insulin is produced at a very low level. In most maturity–onset diabetes, insulin is produced at a normal level or a level much higher than that of the nondiabetic. The highest levels have been found in the more obese. It has been shown that the enlarged fat cells (as in obesity) are resistant to various actions of insulin, including insulin–aided entry of glucose into the cell. This causes the pancreas to secrete ever larger quantities of insulin, and this in turn contributes to obesity. Thus obesity tends to aggravate diabetes and diabetes tends to increase obesity.

Obesity as Disease

Some now consider obesity itself a disease. In 1985 a National Institutes of Health consensus panel declared that obesity is a disease and that "Any degree of overweight, even 5 or 10 pounds, may be hazardous to health. And everyone who is 20 percent or more overweight . . . should make every effort to reduce." However, the accepted ideal weights variances make it almost impossible to determine degrees of obesity as precisely as five or 10 pounds, and the NIH offered no guidelines. They further admitted that it was difficult to determine ideal weights for children because children's weights fluctuate so greatly, and "most fat children grow up to be of normal weight."

Several prominent medical authorities have criticized this consensus report. Dr. William Bennett and Joel Gurin in an article in *The New York Times* call the report "baffling and depressing because it serves no medical purpose and makes quasi–official doctrine out of shaky science and unwarranted speculation."

In the last few years the treatment regimen that has developed from alcohol and drug addiction treatment suggests that obesity caused by overeating, along with other eating disorders, is an addictive disorder.

SOCIAL ASPECTS OF OBESITY
Traditional Attitudes

Societal attitudes about obesity are culturally determined and have varied throughout history. We know, as we shall see in the sections on anorexia nervosa and bulimia, that recent social attitudes about obesity and ideal weights favor the lower end of the ideal weight charts, so much so that some people who are clearly underweight are obsessed with dieting because they feel overweight.

Historically, body weights considered ideal were much greater. Because statistics about heights and weights have only been compiled during this century, it is difficult to compare earlier historical eras with ours in determining relative heights and weights as well as attitudes about what people considered ideal. One insight into ideal weights from the past can be had by looking at art from the period.

Anne Hollander, an art historian, in an article in *The New York Times* said, "The opulent fleshy beauty of Rubens' women probably made the leaner ladies of his day frown when they patted their own meager stomachs, and wish they could compete in the big leagues." Peter Paul Rubens was a late 16th and early 17th century Flemish painter who portrayed distinctly fat beauties. Ms. Hollander further claims, "For about 400 years, roughly between 1500 and 1900, bodily weight and volume, for both men and women, had a strong visual appeal. There were variations according to country and century in this standard of good looks, but in general it was considered not only beautiful but natural to look physically substantial."

Sandro Botticelli, a painter in 15th and 16th century Florence, decorated many of his paintings with cherubim and angels that by today's norms would be considered distinctly chubby. Since the figures in Botticelli's paintings were clearly meant to represent physical beauty, it can be reasonably concluded that what people thought to be ideal body weight was much greater then than now.

Going further back in history to several hundred years B.C., the Ancient Greeks erected statues of gods and heroes, who while not as fat as Rubens' figures, today would be regarded as overweight. Representations of ancient Buddhas and other oriental gods and heroes are clearly obese.

Most attitudes about what constitutes beauty and ideal weights seem to focus mostly on women. For reasons not fully understood, obese men do not suffer from the same social constraints as obese women. They appear not to provoke the intense hostility obese women frequently report. Also most support organizations for the obese are almost entirely populated by women. Few men are found at Weight Watchers meetings and not many more at Overeaters Anonymous. For one thing the structure of Weight Watchers, with its food recipes and diet strategy, seems more naturally geared to women's interests. In addition its magazine has the look and editorial feel of a women's–interest publication, and most articles are about and by women.

One clear reason obesity is less a male issue is that, according to surveys on self–perceptions of obesity, few nonobese men saw themselves as having a weight problem. In contrast in all surveys, a high percentage of nonobese women viewed themselves as having a weight problem.

Anthropologists have reported on attitudes about body weight. In some primitive societies, because it is a mark of plentiful nutrition and diminished physical activity, obesity may be a symbol of status. In Tonga, an archipelago in the Pacific, the monarchs have traditionally been immensely obese. The late queen, mother of the current very obese king, was a highly popular and beloved figure to her people, and her physical carriage and demeanor tended to emphasize her obesity as a badge of rank. The people of Tonga, where some degree of obesity was once considered both beautiful and healthy, have recently begun to adopt attitudes similar to those in developed countries, where obesity is déclassé. *The New York Times* reported that Tonga's current monarch, King Taufaahau Tupou IV, has gone on a diet and numerous Tongans are following his lead. The king is six feet three inches and weighs 360 pounds.

Miss Tonga of 1987, Kerry Crowley, who is five feet nine inches and weighs 133 pounds, said fellow Tongans used to pity her as scrawny and would often remark, "She would be such a pretty girl if only she would gain some weight."

The fear of fat and the distorted concepts of ideal weight may have reached such an impossible ideal of thinness that the pendulum may be swinging back. Increasingly social attitudes about obesity are shifting away from the premise, largely a product of post–World War II America, that everyone must be as thin as possible in order to be healthy, happy and beautiful. The often heard saying, "You can never be too thin or too rich," attributed to various famous people, is increasingly a reminder of the growing realization that one can in fact be "too thin." As anorexia nervosa and bulimia appear to be on the rise as serious medical problems, particularly for young women, attitudes about what body styles constitute beauty and what degree of voluptuousness constitute over-weight might be shifting in a direction away from the idea that "you can never be too thin."

Beginning with Dr. Marcia Millman when she published *Such a Pretty Face* in 1980 and Sharon Greene Patton's *Stop Dieting—Start Living* in 1983, professionals are beginning to recognize not only the medical dangers of radical dieting, but are also challenging the aesthetic assumptions that thin is beautiful and voluptuousness is obesity. However, discrimination against the obese is still rampant.

Discrimination

Even from early childhood, the obese are taunted and harassed. Fat children at school, because they are less adept physically, are the last to be chosen for team sports. They never win beauty contests. Because obesity decreases agility and physical ability, they are sometimes considered lazy. Because most clothes are designed for thin people and do not hang well on the obese frame, the obese may be considered slovenly.

Studies show that even college admissions discriminate against the overweight; being overweight reduces girls' chances of admission by as much as 50% and boys' by as much as one–third.

Another area of discrimination, particularly for overweight women, is in the clothing industry, where fashion is dominated by designers who show their clothes using the thinnest models they can find and who seldom market their clothes in sizes larger than 12, even though more than one–third of American women wear a size 16 or larger. When questioned about why clothes are modeled by extremely thin women, fashion industry representatives reply that designers feel their "designs show up to greater advantage on thin models" where the lines of the clothes are not interrupted by body curves and can hang naturally, supported only at the shoulders. And, to further complicate things, photographers say that people appear to be much fatter in photographs than in real life and so choose the thinnest models.

Such overt discrimination, especially in childhood, may cause the obese, and those who think they are obese, to develop psychological problems in response, thereby compounding the problems they already have from being obese.

In *Such a Pretty Face* Dr. Millman describes case after case in which obese women tell of cruel and insensitive treatment because of their weight. In almost all cases, women experienced direct hostile confrontations about their weight from family members and doctors, as well as the more subtle assaults overheard by chance, such as "that fat slob," or "cow," and remarks directed at them by strangers, the most infamous, oft–repeated and irritating being the remark that served as the title of her book: "My dear, you have such a pretty face. You would be so pretty if only you would lose some weight."

Dr. Millman also describes illogical and apparently inexplicable hostilities of nonobese people when they encounter the obese. Otherwise charitable and kind people find themselves overcome with feelings of disgust and even hatred for casually encountered obese people. They complain that fat people take up more than their share of space, and they drive up insurance rates because they are more prone to medical problems.

One insurance company, Blue Cross, once ran advertisements with the photograph of a massively obese man and accompanying charts pointing out how he and other obese people distort insurance rates.

Surprisingly, many fat women have reported that it is their doctors who are likely to be the most hostile about their obesity. Several women reported that doctors refused to treat them until they lost weight. One woman was refused birth control pills on the grounds that she had high blood pressure. When she pointed out that the nurse had not taken her blood pressure, she was told, "All obese people have high blood pressure."

The striking thing about this treatment of the obese as pariahs is that no one seems to realize that it is bigotry. Often the victims of the bigotry seem not to realize it themselves and develop guilt complexes about being obese that tend to validate society's opinion. They become afraid to go to the beach, to be seen in a bathing suit; women particularly develop fears even of shopping. They have to buy clothes at specialty shops, they are ashamed to be seen buying food. Dr. Millman describes one woman who, when she shopped for food, would buy only one or two items in one store, then shop in another for a few other items, all so she would not appear to be a glutton.

TREATMENT OF OBESITY

There are numerous treatment regimens for obesity, many of dubious benefit; however, the major approaches are medical treatment, camps and spas, support groups and self–help.

Medical Treatment

The medical treatment of obesity can involve simple procedures such as dieting supervised by doctors or hospital personnel to serious major surgery.

Typically, both diet specialists, who are usually MDs, and treatment centers recruit patients through newspaper ads. On any given day in a large city daily newspaper, three or four display ads will appear on the back page of the "Living," "Home" or "Fashion' section of the paper. For example, in the *Dallas Morning News* for October 10, 1988, three such ads appear. All promise quick weight loss; one promises no pills or injections; one promises no prepackaged foods; one features the Medifast trademark, which is prepackaged food; one offers a guarantee; and one hints at insurance reimbursement.

It is estimated that there are 2,000 such treatment programs across the country. Some are private doctors and some are associated with hospitals. Treatment is expensive, about $500 per month in most cases for once–a–week outpatient consultation. Residential programs range in cost from a low of about $6,000 per month to a high of about $30,000, with the usual program lasting from four to six weeks. The outpatient program usually features prepackaged diet foods such as liquid or powdered proteins, sometimes a combination of solid food and formula, which the patient takes for about 12 weeks. This is a modified fast that may provide only 400 to 800 calories per day, depending on the size of the patient, the patient's health and the rate at which the patient wants to lose weight. After the fast, a "refeeding" program is introduced along with a behavior modification program designed to maintain desirable weight.

In evaluating these programs, researchers have found that use of behavior modification programs seems to improve the success rate. In one study in which some subjects had dieted with a behavior modification program and some had dieted without, it was found that after three years the failure to maintain weight loss was 9% less for those who participated in behavior modification; in other words, behavior modification improved success by 9%. Behavior modification programs are more often found at the residential programs, which are more intensive and expensive, than at the weekly programs, which mostly stress diet management and the taking of diet supplements.

Dr. Theodore B. Van Itallie, formerly at the Obesity Research Center at St. Luke's–Roosevelt Hospital Center in New York, was quoted by *The New York Times* regarding these programs: ". . . morbidly obese individuals can tolerate very low-calorie diets (providing 300 to 500 calories per day) far better than moderately obese persons can." Dr. Van Itallie criticized the medical profession for using the diets indiscriminately without considering the varying needs of the individual, such as body size and activity levels, as well as whether or not the resulting weight loss is composed of mostly fat or mostly lean body mass. "What people who run these diets don't talk about is the people who go into emergency rooms with all kinds of symptoms." Some symptoms include dehydration, dizziness and fainting, inability to tolerate cold, diarrhea, constipation, dry skin, hair loss and a buildup of uric acid that can cause gout.

Durham, North Carolina, appears to be the diet capital of the world with four major treatment centers, two associated with the Duke University medical school and another a spinoff of the Duke programs. One is based on Dr. Walter Kempner's rice diet developed in the 1940s to treat cardiovascular and kidney problems. The Durham Chamber of Commerce estimates that the clinics are a $12 million per year business for the city, and that clients generate about $40 million annually for the Durham economy. Fees for the Durham clinics range from about $1,000 to almost $2,000 per month and do not include residential accommodations. The clinics attract a number of celebrities such as Marilyn Horne and the late James Coco.

Some newer treatment facilities, such as Shades of Hope at Buffalo Gap, Texas, are residential programs, not to be confused with spas or weight loss camps. Many of these programs' treatment approaches are modeled after alcohol treatment. The counselors at these centers regard all eating disorders as addictions, and treatment is structured accordingly. Various psychotherapy techniques are employed in treatment, frequently in group settings. A group technique known as "family sculpting" is used in which the client being treated asks others in the group to act out being someone important in the client's development process, usually parents and siblings. The "family members" are given scripts, usually a few words or sentences the client remembers the real family members frequently saying that may have had an early negative impact on the client's development. While the "family members" say their scripts, the client says all that he was unable to express to the real family member. For example, a mother might frequently have told her child, "You will never amount to anything." In family sculpting, the child is able to refute the mother, forgive her and begin a healing process.

Many other therapy techniques are used in an effort to restore or build self–esteem, forgive past destructive behavior and focus on developing new behavioral habits. Treatment centers also teach good nutrition, sensible cooking and eating habits known as "gentle eating," in which food is savored for the pleasure of nourishing hunger rather than as a focus of compulsive habit.

Clients are introduced to the 12–step program of Overeaters Anonymous and in aftercare programs are encouraged to begin a lifelong commitment to the OA program.

In addition to the usual addiction–treatment therapy, a relatively new disorder known as codependency and widely associated with addictive disorders is also treated. Therapy for codependency and addiction assumes the patient needs orientation, not only in respect to his own behavior, but also in respect to family and group systems in which he lives. Family members of clients, many of whom are codependent, are encouraged to participate in this therapy. It is assumed to do little good to modify the behavior of the overeater if his family does not alter its behavior to add support. Therapists point out that spouses, parents and others in relationship with the overeater must all modify their behavior in concert in order for treatment to be effective and lasting. Family members especially, through negative comments, selfish needs or for other perverse reasons, frequently and subtly encourage the overeater to overeat and the alcoholic to drink.

Surgery

Surgery is reserved for the massively or morbidly obese or for those who because of their obesity are at a grave health risk. There are two major surgical procedures: liposuction or suction lipectomy, and intestinal bypass surgery.

Liposuction, a procedure that employs the use of a suction tool inserted into the subcutaneous fat layer, literally sucks fat from the body. This is considered a dangerous operation and several deaths have resulted. It began as a treatment for massive obesity, but it has recently come to be thought of largely as a cosmetic surgery technique that allows surgeons to "sculpt" the body. Specialists are now in a controversy over whether cosmetic surgeons, who are now performing a large portion of liposuction procedures, should be allowed to perform the surgery or whether it should be a last resort procedure for people who are so obese that their lives are threatened.

Another surgery technique, bypass surgery, creates a loop that bypasses portions of both the large and the small intestine and reduces the amount of food absorbed; thus weight loss is assured even while overeating. This too is a dangerous operation, and deaths have resulted from it. It is reserved for the massively obese whose lives are threatened by their weight. Thus far, this procedure is not being performed by cosmetic surgeons.

A technique called gastroplasty was introduced in the early 1980s in which a portion of the stomach is stapled, limiting the amount of food that can be taken. While no deaths have been directly linked to this procedure, it is too early to tell if it might have any lasting effect on weight loss.

Camps and Spas

Camps and spas are similar, generally camps being for children and spas for adults. Children's weight loss camps are very much like any other children's camp, except for the special emphasis on weight loss. In fact many overweight children going to regular summer camps experience weight loss because of the heightened physical activity. However, weight loss camps concentrate on diet and on teaching improved nutrition, better eating habits and moderation in addition to usual children's camp activities of crafts and sports.

Spas, a grownup version of the weight loss camp, are usually found in luxurious surroundings, once mostly in rural settings, but now increasingly in urban areas, usually as part of resort hotels.

The spa program works as a highly regimented short–term, quick weight loss program and is only peripherally if at all connected with any kind of medical establishment, although there are always consulting physicians, nutritionists and dietitians available. Spa clients are given a low calorie diet somewhat similar to those of diet treatment centers, although more palatable. In addition clients are provided rigorous exercise regimens: aerobics, swimming, sometimes hiking and tennis. Clients spend one to two weeks in residence at the spas. They are encouraged not to leave the premises during their stay in order to prevent going off their starvation diets.

Spa clients are rarely massively obese; some are even quite thin. Almost all are rich. The lowest spa rates are about $2,000 per week and the average is around $5,000 to $6,000 per week, not reimbursed by insurance. Exceptions are the Weight Watchers camps and spas, which are a combination of camps and spas serving both children and adults and tending to be less expensive; however, because Weight Watchers licenses rather than franchises private camps the styles, accommodations and costs vary.

Support Groups

There are numerous organizations devoted to problems of the obese, most of them covered in the chapter on organizations. However the three most notable groups are National Association to Aid Fat Americans (NAAFA), Overeaters Anonymous and Weight Watchers.

NAAFA differs from most support groups because its goals are not to encourage weight loss, rather to provide support and fight discrimination. Its members are mostly women, and its activities center around meetings and social events. It sponsors dances at which members are able to socialize and meet members of the opposite sex. These dances attract men who are attracted to obese women.

NAAFA members lobby for anti–discrimination laws and publicize economic discrimination against the obese. The NAAFA newsletter reviews books relating to obesity, has articles about new obesity treatments and lists resources such as places to buy clothes and doctors sympathetic to fat people.

History and Treatment

Overeaters Anonymous (OA) is a support organization modeled very closely on Alcoholics Anonymous (AA). It has adapted AA's famous 12 steps to apply to overeaters. The 12 steps take the participants from the initial admission of being powerless over eating, through a series of steps that bring themselves and their eating habits into control.

OA members attend meetings in which they testify about their problems, not only about eating but also about all elements of their lives that have an impact on their emotional state, and thus their eating habits. They offer each other support, both at the meeting and in private personal relationships. Each member has a sponsor who provides support and is available for consultation and encouragement at any hour of day or night. As the member progresses in the program, he in turn sponsors newer members.

OA eating goals are to establish rational eating habits based on programs the overeaters devise themselves: some may cut out snacking and bingeing, others may eat many small meals in a day. OA regards overeating as a lifelong problem without a cure, and views its own program as requiring lifetime commitment.

Weight Watchers is probably the best known support organization. Its focus is on weight reduction and maintenance through carefully controlled dieting and eating habits. At meetings participants talk about psychological problems they feel underlie their overeating. In addition to licensing camps and spas, they have also licensed their name to a line of diet foods found in supermarkets throughout the country. They publish a monthly magazine, *Weight Watchers*, which features inspirational stories about successfully dealing with problems with overweight.

Self–Help

Self–help in dealing with obesity is frequently limited to dieting, and sometimes dieting combined with exercise. With the possible exception of the eating disorder treatment centers that treat overeating as an addiction, it is known that the overall success rate of any weight loss program is only 5%; therefore, except for those who are morbidly obese or have medical problems related to obesity, engaging in self–help programs probably offers the same prospect of weight loss as some of the more sophisticated and costly methods. However, it is also more dangerous because unsupervised dieting can lead to major medical problems.

Overweight people frequently report that they are always on one self–imposed diet or another because, if for no other reason, it seems to make their obesity more acceptable to those around them if they are seen as "doing something about it." Experts are increasingly coming to agree that self–imposed weight loss programs can be harmful.

There are other, more dangerous, self–induced weight loss methods, which are themselves eating disorders: anorexia nervosa and bulimia, which are dealt with in the next section.

Self-Imposed Diets:

The term "fad diet" is used increasingly in discussing self–imposed dieting experiences. As used it is clearly a derogatory term, implying that people go on a diet when it is popular, then abandon it or switch to a newer, more fashionable diet. That is precisely what happens, and that demonstrates one of the major reasons self–imposed or fad diets usually don't work. Often fad diets published in women's magazines and in books may be based on sound nutritional advice, and following them will produce weight loss; however, the problem obese people have with dieting is not losing weight but in maintaining a lower weight after initial dieting. Most fad diets tout "quick weight loss" and the idea that once the dieter has achieved an ideal weight, he will be able to abandon the diet and maintain the weight loss.

Authors of the diets and even physicians who prescribe diets point out that the diets are sound—if followed rigidly they will produce weight loss—but the dieters fail to follow them for a sufficient length of time to achieve success. Nevertheless, their 95% failure rate demonstrates that there are other, more complex reasons for obesity than can be easily addressed simply through the process of dieting, whether they are physician prescribed, or the latest eating fads as presented in popular magazines and books.

All fad diets are based on reducing caloric intake—all weight loss programs not involving exercise are—but some employ gimmicks suggesting that the dieter can eat as much as he wants and still lose weight; and he can, as long as "as much as he wants" does not exceed the caloric limits of the diet.

While some self–imposed diets are just sensible nutrition with greatly reduced portions, some are actually dangerous because they depend on creating imbalances within the body to achieve weight loss. One example is the once popular low carbohydrate diet, which promised the dieter as much protein, such as meat and eggs, as he could eat as long as he cut out high carbohydrate foods such as bread and vegetables. This created an imbalance in such essential elements as fiber and vitamins. Also carbohydrates are an important element in production of energy. Energy is burned in the body as glucose, which is most readily converted from carbohydrates. When carbohydrates are absent from the diet, the body steals protein from muscles to convert to energy. Much of the subcutaneous fat remains right where it is, under the skin.

Some of the popular diets that have come and gone with little or no lasting results include Calories Don't Count, Quick Weight Loss Diet, Diet Revolution, Scarsdale Diet, The Beverly Hills Diet, The Southampton Diet, and countless other less well–known diet books. There is almost always a diet book on *The New York Times* bestseller list, which sells until the next diet book is released and replaces it on the list.

Another form of self–imposed dieting once involved the purchase of liquid protein over the counter, now largely restricted to doctor supervised dieting. On this diet the dieter stops eating altogether, getting all his nutrients from the liquid, which works on the same principle as the low carbohydrate diet, its essential element being the restriction of carbohydrate intake. The dangers are similar to the low carbohydrate diets, and the liquid diets were immensely popular until several deaths were reported. Among the more popular liquid diets were Metracal and the Cambridge Diet, which was a liquid system featuring 330 calories a day and was sold through mail order to dieters, who were then induced to sell it to friends for a commission. Liquid diets were so popular that only two years after they had been introduced, total retail sales for that one diet product alone reached $150,000,000 per year.

In 1982 the Food and Drug Administration (FDA) issued a statement blaming several deaths and more hospitalizations on various liquid diets. The Centers for Disease Control (CDC) has recently concluded that these deaths were likely the result of starvation.

Weight Loss Gimmicks and Appliances:

In addition to fad diets and liquid diets, other weight loss gimmicks, some originating in a serious effort to solve the problems of obesity but many others just clever marketing schemes, have included hormone shots, low–calorie sweeteners, a medical procedure that wires the mouth shut and "spot–reducing" machines such as Relax–a–cisor, which pummeled the fat away while the patient slept. Amphetamines, once prescribed as an appetite suppressant, reached sales of $80,000,000 per year before being discontinued as a weight control method. Today, an unknown quantity of amphetamines are still in use as an underground attempt at weight reduction. One hormone treatment sold over–the–counter, steroidal hormone DHEA, was withdrawn by the FDA because it had never been approved for weight loss treatment. Virtually all of these procedures were ineffective and some were even dangerous.

Recently a procedure was developed using a balloon device, called the Garren–Edwards Gastric Bubble, which was placed in the stomach to reduce food intake by producing feelings of satiety. However, the procedure was abruptly halted when several deaths resulted.

The concept of "cellulite"—fat cells that have been transformed from ordinary fat into especially hard–to–reduce substances and deposited in particularly conspicuous parts of the body such as the hips, especially women's hips—promised to be a fad of its own. Its stock faded, but appears to have arisen again. Linda Wells, in her *New York Times Magazine* beauty column of July 3, 1988, reported that

> The term [cellulite] is not a medical one, but rather a catchall way of identifying flabby dimpled skin on the thighs and buttocks . . . recently creams and massaging tools to battle cellulite have moved into department–store cosmetic counters, where many companies are envisioning profit potential. According to estimates by some cosmetic companies, more than 90 percent of all American women have cellulite.

Cellulite products now available include Elancyl MP24 Body Profiling Concentrate, Biotherm's 10 Day Body Contouring Treatment Kit and Revlon's Respirar 02 Aqua Problem Zones Gel, complete with a body roller. According to Ms. Wells, "The Anushka Institute in New York City . . . charges $575 for 10 sessions, which include nutritional guidance, electronic muscle stimulation, body wraps and treatments with two kinds of sea weed imported from France." Ever–hopeful weight loss consumers spend millions of dollars annually on these and other equally ridiculous treatments.

TRENDS FOR THE FUTURE

The only clear trend in the understanding and treatment of obesity seems to be growing agreement that most current treatments, for whatever combination of reasons, fail. A growing body of experts as well as a number of the obese themselves—represented by growing organizations such as the National Association to Aid Fat Americans—are beginning to advise the vast majority of those considered obese not to diet. Instead they are calling for a redefinition, not so much of obesity in its extreme forms, but of where obesity begins and where normal weights leave off.

There is no disagreement about the effects of morbid obesity and the need for treatment. Treatment is becoming more complex and is beginning to factor in behavior modification as an essential element. Moreover, the complex family and social systems in which the obese live are increasingly being pulled into the newer treatments, such as those offered by the Rader Institutes, a chain of treatment centers housed in hospitals throughout the country, and the smaller intimate residential centers like Shades of Hope in Buffalo Gap, Texas.

Fad diets and weight loss gimmicks have not gone away. Only time will reveal how far the new understanding of obesity will filter into widely held aesthetic beliefs about ideals of weight and beauty.

ANOREXIA NERVOSA

INTRODUCTION

Anorexia nervosa is a puzzling and frustrating disorder—to the anorectic herself, her family and the care givers attempting to provide therapy and physical treatment. The physical cure for anorexia nervosa is simply to eat, something almost everyone on earth enjoys, including the anorectic. However, the anorectic is so afraid of becoming obese and has such a distorted image of her body, that she steadfastly refuses to eat even when ravenously hungry.

As more is being learned about this disorder, family, teachers, doctors and anorectics themselves are beginning to benefit from the experience of recovered and recovering anorectics, and therapeutic trends are becoming clearer.

DEFINING ANOREXIA

Anorexia nervosa is a form of self–starvation leading to extreme emaciation, usually resulting from a morbid fear of becoming fat or of losing control of one's eating behavior. The word *anorexia*, first used to describe the condition by English physician Sir William Gull in 1873, means "lack of appetite," however, anorectics do not lack appetite, but on the contrary are obsessed with thoughts of food.

Primary, or "restrictive," anorectics achieve and maintain their low weight through fasting and sometimes through excessive exercise.

Other anorectics, now more often called bulimarexics, may maintain low weight by vomiting after eating, or they may take laxatives or drugs in addition to fasting.

DIAGNOSING ANOREXIA

Diagnostic Criteria

The diagnostic criteria for anorexia nervosa, according to the *Diagnostic and Statistical Manual of Mental Disorders*, 3rd edition (DSM III) of the American Psychiatric Association are:

A. Intense fear of becoming obese, which does not diminish as weight loss progresses
B. Disturbance of body image, e.g., claiming to "feel fat" even when emaciated
C. Weight loss of at least 25% of original body weight or, if under 18 years of age, weight loss from original body weight plus projected weight

gain expected from growth charts may be combined to make the 25%
D. Refusal to maintain body weight over a minimal normal weight for
age and height
E. No known physical illness that would account for the weight loss.

Hilde Bruch, in *The Golden Cage*, describes pre–illness features of anorectic youngsters as "first, severe disturbance in the body image, the way they see themselves; second, misinterpretations of internal and external stimuli, with inaccuracy in the way hunger is experienced as the most pronounced symptom; and third, a paralyzing underlying sense of ineffectiveness, the conviction of being helpless to change anything about their lives." However, many eating disorder treatment professionals regard anorexia as being a symptom of underlying psychological disorders as well as being an eating disorder in itself. According to Tennie Mc-Carty, director of Shades of Hope treatment center in Buffalo Gap, Texas, anorectics, along with compulsive overeaters and bulimics, almost always begin to reveal underlying issues of codependency and other psychological dysfunctions during the early course of treatment. Treatment focus must then shift to focus on these previously deeply hidden issues.

Visual diagnosis of anorexia, or the presenting symptom, usually relies on the degree of emaciation. Using the Metropolitan Life height and weight tables as a guide, experts say anorexia begins at about 25% below ideal body weights listed in the tables. Thus a woman 5 feet 9 inches weighing 100 pounds or less and having no physical reason for emaciation such as cancer, other prolonged illness or other psychological illness such as severe depression would be regarded as anorectic.

Although most anorectics, about 60%, maintain their low weight through diet restriction and exercise, some anorectics engage in bingeing and purging (excessive eating followed by vomiting), and in that regard resemble bulimics.

Physical Features of Anorexia

In the process of emaciation the insulating layer of fat is diminished, resulting in sensitivity to cold and heat. The skin dries and the extremities become cold, often appearing blue. The hair becomes brittle, and a soft downy hair, called lanugo, begins to appear in unexpected parts of the body such as the back, face and arms. The heart beat slows and blood pressure diminishes. Metabolism slows to accommodate the diminished food intake, much as it does in hibernating animals and in people suffering famine. The stools diminish and constipation is common. Edema (fluid retention) may occur, especially when attempts are made to regain weight, and that in turn may trigger new reducing efforts by the anorectic.

Another important characteristic of anorexia in post–pubescent women is the cessation of menses. Dental problems may also develop. Action of acid on the teeth from repeated vomiting may erode dental enamel, and dehydration reduces saliva production, also contributing to decay.

As many as 20% of anorectics may die from suicide, malnutrition or other causes such as diminished immune responses that allow infection to take hold or electrolyte imbalance, which in turn can produce heart arrhythmias.

WHO ARE THE ANORECTIC?

Unlike many psychological disorders that are more or less equally distributed throughout the population as a whole, striking both male and female, rich and poor, typical anorectics tend to share many common characteristics: anorexia usually begins in adolescence near the onset of puberty; it strikes most heavily in affluent families; and it is overwhelmingly a disorder of females, with females being 15 times more likely to become anorectic than males. However, increasingly cases of anorexia onset at ages as late as 59 are being reported. Studies indicate that as many as one in 100 teenage girls and young women suffer from the disorder to one degree or another. Anorexia has not been found in underdeveloped countries where food is scarce.

CAUSES OF ANOREXIA

Psychological Causes

Psychologists, notably Hilde Bruch, believe anorexia to be the result of psychological disturbance, pointing out that the symptoms of anorexia—self–starvation, emaciation and bingeing and purging—come late in the progression of whatever disorders underlie anorexia. The major psychological features seem to be the fear of maturing and the fear of loss of control.

An article in *The New York Times* magazine by Sam Blum quotes Dr. Orestes Arcuni of the Payne Whitney Clinic in New York,

> *Put simply . . . the child with anorexia nervosa is trying desperately not to grow up. Her body is becoming a woman's, against her will. That's got to be stopped. It's more terrifying than the logical fact that if she doesn't eat, she'll die, because she's experiencing it at a far more primitive level . . . although a child generally learns that he is a separate entity from his mother by the time he is 1 year old, it*

takes until he is 18 months or so before he is ready to begin the process of physically moving away from her . . . a mother might not be able to tolerate it that this baby that she'd been raising and holding to her breast, clutching for the first year of its life, is starting to move away from her. And unintentionally she conveys the feeling that any self–assertion is dangerous; it hurts her; it might hurt her so badly that she'll withdraw her love and support . . . So he tries to stifle his 2–year–old rebelliousness. He'll continue to develop, to grow, but only according to his mother's directions.

According to Bruch and other experts, issues of dominance and control progress from these early childhood experiences until the onset of puberty, when growth and maturity become difficult to ignore. Control issues then focus on the body, and the child begins restricting eating when she discovers that body weight is the one aspect of growth she can control.

Pam Estes, a therapist specializing in the treatment of eating disorders, says, "More and more, we are beginning to find similarities in the family dynamics of anorectics and bulimics. Both tend to have overcontrolling mothers and intimate and enmeshed fathers. Parents also tend to demand perfection of their anorectic and bulimic children."

Cherry Boone O'Neill, daughter of singer Pat Boone, in her book *Starving for Attention* describes the "good–little–girl syndrome," in which she strove for an impossible perfection. She also describes the intolerable pressures felt by anorectics, "as our family act became more popular, keeping up with schoolwork was becoming a real challenge; my life was slipping more and more out of my control. It seemed I was being constantly dictated to by people and circumstances . . ."

Bruch believes self–starvation is a late and perhaps secondary development in the course of the syndrome, which may be primarily issues of control and "a sense of identity, competence and effectiveness." Anorectics typically exhibit confusion regarding body image, seeing themselves as fat even when emaciated, and are unable to interpret body signals such as hunger, sexual feelings and emotions. They have feelings of ineffectiveness and helplessness.

Social pressures are thought to be a major contributor to the onset of anorexia, particularly relating to the rapidly changing roles of women in society. Bruch has also suggested that depression and other psychiatric disturbances arising after puberty are contributing factors.

Biological Causes

Some researchers think there may be biological causes for anorexia as well as psychological. In some cases cessation of menstruation—one of the indicators of anorexia—has occurred before the onset of anorexia, suggesting that some biological factor might trigger the cessation of menses, and thus trigger anorexia. Research into biological causes is ongoing. Until about the mid–1950s doctors thought anorexia was caused by a malfunction of the pituitary gland, and they treated it, without success, with hormones.

Researchers think some anorexia nervosa may be caused by a malfunctioning hypothalamus, a gland that produces hormones and regulates hunger, thirst and temperature and also regulates endocrine glands, including thyroid, adrenal and pituitary glands, as well as testes and ovaries.

Onset of Anorexia Nervosa

Often the onset is thought to be a disturbed self–image, aggravated by social pressures to be thin, and the developmental conflicts arising at the onset of puberty. Dr. Bruch states in *The Golden Cage*, "The enigma of anorexia nervosa is how successful and well–functioning families fail to transmit an adequate sense of confidence and self–value to these children. They grow up confused in their concepts about the body and its functions and deficient in their sense of identity, autonomy and control." Dr. Bruch has also suggested that eating patterns in infancy may influence the later onset of anorexia.

Many anorectics begin their self–starvation at some point of developmental crisis in maturity such as when moving with family to a new home, changing schools and leaving friends behind or going away to college. Others appear to stumble upon anorexia during the process of dieting to correct obesity. Some have reported feelings of lack of control, particularly in regard to eating, and found that self–starvation was a response to being out of control. Many recovering anorectics claim that they were surprised and gratified that they had found something that restored some sense of control.

Many anorectics remember some particular crisis that appeared to precipitate some aspect of the anorectic's destructive behavior. Cherry Boone O'Neill discovered vomiting as a weight control technique after her mother flushed all her stolen diet pills down the toilet. "Once my dietary crutches were kicked out from under me, I set out with single–minded determination to design a rigid regimen to insure myself against gorging. But my willpower was gradually fading . . . The loss of my diet pills and self–discipline unleashed a seemingly insatiable appetite and my eating went virtually unchecked." Fearing weight gain, she vomited regularly after eating.

SOCIAL ASPECTS OF ANOREXIA: THINNESS
AS BEAUTY
Social Pressures to Be Thin

Discussions of the psychological factors in the cause of anorexia pointing to the need to be in control, the fear of growing up and other psychological factors do not explain why the incidence of anorexia is on the increase and why it is unknown in countries where famine and low food supply are common. Presumably the psychological factors relating to anorexia's underlying causes existed in the past and continue to exist in countries where anorexia is not known. This would strongly indicate that social pressures to be thin is a strong trigger that catapults young women already prone to be influenced by social ideals of beauty and acceptable weight norms into extreme behavior that in other times and other societies would find expression in other psychological disorders. This can probably best be explained by the results of the *Glamour* survey described in the earlier section on obesity in which 45% of underweight respondents felt themselves too fat and needing to lose weight. In other words, the growing fashion toward extreme thinness exerts its own taboos on those most strongly within the grips of fashion: the affluent, females, the young. These same factors torture and punish the obese for their inability to lose weight; others become anorectic when they push themselves into extremes of weight loss in order to avoid becoming social pariahs.

In the past before thinness was fashionable there were no social pressures to be thin. On the contrary, extremely thin people were regarded as being ill and in poor health. In underdeveloped countries, thin people are commonplace, not because of social pressures, but because of the scarcity of food and the prevalence of debilitating diseases.

The exaggerated need for mother's approval of the child cited by Dr. Arcuni is replaced by the equally immature and exaggerated need for society's approval in the older adolescent and young adult.

Sir William Gull, who first described and named anorexia nervosa, was one of the physicians who attended Queen Victoria and her family. Gull treated upper class and upper middle class patients, and he described the symptoms of anorexia nervosa as being similar to hysteria, a common description of psychological disturbance of women at that time, but coined the term "nervosa" because he also observed the disorder in males.

When Cherry Boone O'Neill, on a day when school pictures were being made, first realized that she was becoming overweight, she cried all afternoon. In her book *Starving for Attention* she says,

> *That was D–Day for me, the day the diet began. My hatred of fat had escalated into a stark fury and this furious hatred of my fat translated into a furious hatred of myself. That very moment I made a commitment that I was going to shed those ugly pounds regardless of the cost. I'll starve if I have to, I thought, but I am going to regain control over my eating and my body even if it kills me!*

Dr. Arcuni has described the need for approval in this way:

> *Perhaps nothing is more agreed upon in the literature of anorexia nervosa—and it is vast—than that, before 'getting sick,' the children had been astonishingly good, the envy of other parents. They would not only eat what was set before them, they'd dress according to their mother's tastes, never talk back, never display anger at brothers or sisters, never say no . . . Outwardly compliant and charming, inside the children were seething but terrified 2–year–olds.*
>
> *In adolescence this adaptation to life can lead to a psychiatric condition labeled 'borderline.' One might live as an appendage of mother throughout childhood, but there is no denying at adolescence that one is becoming a person separate from mother . . . Yet to the emotionally arrested 2–year–old within, to grow up and away from mother is still to be deserted and die. The individual, faced with such an unresolved conflict, seems to have the "choice" of becoming schizophrenic or putting up some sort of fight for control.*

That fight for control, although it can take many other forms, such as disruptive behavior or drug addiction, is what, in many cases, leads to anorexia.

Early Warning Signs of Anorexia

Dr. Paul Garfinkel, in the *Harvard Medical School Health Letter*, suggests several signs parents, teachers and doctors should be aware of:

Changing weight goals. When a young woman (or, much less frequently, man) reaches a weight loss goal and immediately sets a new, lower goal, the potential for developing anorexia is high.

Dieting in isolation. Dieting is generally a social activity in our culture. Dieters tend to hang out or compare notes with other dieters. Determined dieting pursued in isolation should be regarded warily.

Dissatisfaction with success. Most dieters regard lost pounds with delight. When a successful dieter remains self–critical, she should be watched.

Amenorrhea. When menstruation ceases, anorexia nervosa may be imminent or may already have developed.

TREATMENT OF ANOREXIA

Hospitalization

Hospitalization is the frontline emergency treatment for anorexia, with psychotherapy either following immediately or beginning during hospitalization. Many doctors treat anorexia as an emergency—as in many cases it is when victims and their parents deny the condition until a medical crisis erupts that makes further denial impossible, and they seek hospital treatment.

Some hospitals employ forced feeding techniques, using a feeding tube as well as intravenous feeding in order to force anorectics to gain weight; however, some doctors feel that is counterproductive and simply pushes the anorectic into greater determination to gain control of her eating once hospitalization is ended. Others however, point out that many anorectics are in danger of death by the time they are hospitalized, and forced feeding is essential to insure they do not die before psychotherapy can begin. Moreover, they argue, the patient in a condition of starvation is incapable of making choices, even of choosing to eat in order to save her life.

Dr. Frederick Mittleman, writing in *Anorexia Nervosa: Finding the Lifeline* by Patricia Stein and Barbara Unell, believes anorectics whose body weight is 75% of the ideal should be hospitalized, and if possible, choosing hospitalization should be up to the patient, "even when I fear for the individual's safety. In my opinion, treatment is not successful unless the decision is the individual's. This gives the anorectic some control—something she or he badly needs."

Dr. Mittleman recommends a multidimensional treatment plan involving a physician, nurses, dietician and psychological and occupational counselors. This plan sets specific goals about what the patient should eat, how much and how much weight should be gained, usually about one–half pound per day. If weight goals are not met, liquid supplements are added. The patient eats in the presence of a nurse and is monitored for at least one hour after eating to prevent vomiting. This "refeeding" program is highly structured and not subject to negotiation with the patient. If its results are not satisfactory, he then recommends tube feeding and, as a last resort, hyperalimentation (feeding complete nutrition through the veins), a technique rarely used.

While it is important for the patient to be weighed daily while in the hospital in order to monitor progress, the patient is not normally told her weight, because on a daily basis, weight fluctuations are meaningless and might vary by as much as two or three pounds over just a few days. In follow–up treatment patients are encouraged to weigh themselves no more than once a week in order to help direct the patient's attention away from obsessive weight watching.

An initial target weight for treatment is frequently the weight at which menstruation will return (for a woman who is five feet eight inches, about 116 pounds).

Residential Treatment Facilities

Several pioneering residential treatment programs have been developed during the last few years. The Payne Whitney Clinic at New York Hospital is one; another is the Philadelphia Child Guidance Clinic, affiliated with the Children's Hospital of Philadelphia and the University of Pennsylvania School of Medicine. Many hospitals, such as the Payne Whitney Clinic, recommend prolonged hospitalization—at Payne Whitney, as long as two months—during which the patient is fed and monitored until past the immediate dangers posed by being severely underweight. Counseling may begin during hospitalization and usually continues until the anorexia is under control. The Payne Whitney Clinic also sees discharged patients for as much as a year afterwards in order to monitor medical and physical progress.

One treatment facility, Four Winds, at Katonah, New York uses family therapy and psychodrama, in which patients act out situations they are otherwise unable to describe and resolve. In other therapy at the facility, activities are introduced to patients who may have missed out on them at the appropriate age or may not have been able to experience them within the patient's own family. For example, one adolescent was allowed a pajama party; others are read to at bedtime. Some patients have previously experienced role reversal within their families, in which they have acted the parent to their own parent's role as children and consequently have missed out on an important part of childhood, playtime. Such children often become "perfect," turning away from peers and family, becoming isolated and concentrating on weight control as the central focus of their perfection.

Kangaroo Pump:

The kangaroo pump is used in some residential treatment facilities and hospitals to pump as many as 2,000 calories a day into anorectic patients. Originally devised to feed post–operative patients who have had stomach surgery, the pump was adapted for use in anorexia nervosa by Steven Levenkron, a psychotherapist and author of the book *The Best Little Girl in the World*.

The pump, somewhat like an intravenous feeding device, is suspended from a pole above the patient, and the food, called isocal—a complete liquid diet—is transported through a tube that goes into the patient's nose, down the throat and into the small intestine.

Behavior Modification and Counseling:
In a typical hospital or residential regimen, the patient gradually learns to take responsibility for her own weight gain as she attends group therapy sessions and begins to be allowed mild exercise. As she begins to gain weight she is rewarded by being allowed privileges such as television and increased freedom. Nursing staffs have learned to be wary in monitoring patient's weight gains. Many anorectics, like alcoholics who learn many ingenious ways to find and drink alcohol even while sequestered, may employ similar behavior to avoid gaining weight while convincing nurses they are complying with the program; for example, if not monitored they may stuff food into their pockets or fold it into napkins, flush it down the toilet or drink large amounts of water before being weighed.

It is important for care givers to teach the patient what to expect during the process of refeeding. During the initial stages or regaining weight the patient's stomach may bulge and the patient may have a feeling of being overstuffed. If she is not reassured that this is normal and that the bulge will subside, the anorectic may become alarmed that she is stuffing herself and losing control. This may lead to relapse.

Behavior modification therapy works best when the entire family participates, and both the anorectic and her family can relearn and re–experience important developmental milestones that will allow the anorectic to gain maturity and age–appropriate behavior.

Self–help

Self–help is not recommended for anorexia as it invariably fails. Moreover, because one of the diagnostic criteria for anorexia is a distorted self–image, the anorectic has no point of reference on which to base a self–help regimen, and unfortunately, once the anorectic's weight is spiraling downward, she may feel a tremendous sense of accomplishment and if left unimpeded, will happily continue dieting until she dies.

It may be that some borderline anorectics are able to maintain a stable weight through their own efforts. However, because only very severe cases of anorexia are usually diagnosed, the borderline cases almost never come into treatment, and so technically the borderline case is not an anorectic. Individual efforts by those who successfully maintain a relatively low weight without ever reaching the threshold of 75% of ideal body weight are not considered candidates for treatment.

Group Therapy and Support Groups

Group therapy and support groups are risky because anorexia is "catching." Many therapists report problems of competition among members of therapy groups in which, for example, a patient weighing 80 pounds encounters another patient weighing 70 pounds. The 80–pound patient may become jealous and attempt to reduce further, an effect exactly the opposite of the intent of group therapy.

Linda Lynander, writing in *The New York Times* reports on the experience of the American Anorexia Nervosa Association support group. At one time, the group met once a week until it became so competitive with each member wanting to be the thinnest present that they reduced meetings to once a month. The monthly meetings allow less opportunity for competition and are able to focus on discussion of problems more productively.

Treatment Outcomes

The initial goal of treatment is to achieve a normal weight range for the patient of between 90 and 110% of the ideal body weight according to the height and weight charts. About 70% of anorectic patients in treatment can be expected to achieve those goals after treatment of about six months.

Between 15 and 25% of anorectic patients, particularly those who binge eat, will relapse intermittently; another 15 to 20% continue to be anorectic and may require continuing therapy. Estimates of the number of those who eventually die from the syndrome vary between 10 and 20%. Some die of heart arrhythmias brought on by electrolyte imbalance, caused by excessive vomiting; others die when infections and disease overpower their weakened immune systems; some commit suicide; and some simply starve themselves to death.

BULIMIA

INTRODUCTION

Bulimia was once thought to be a manifestation of anorexia nervosa. Certainly, there is a close relationship between anorexia nervosa and bulimia; some anorectics have bulimic episodes and some bulimics are anorectic, and perhaps some suffer from both disorders equally. Some of the personality characteristics of typical anorectics and bulimics seem to be similar, although others seem to appear in only one or the other disorder.

Before the 1980s bulimia was almost unknown as a named disorder. Even doctors were unaware of it. One bulimia victim tells of being brought to the emergency room of a major teaching hospital. When she told the resident attending her that she had bulimia, the resident replied, "What's that?" Until the disorder began to receive widespread publicity beginning in the early 1980s many women suffering from bulimia believed their disorder to be totally unique to themselves. Most didn't even know it had a name; many reported a great sense of relief to learn both that their suffering had a name and could be described and that they were not alone in their illness but that others suffered the same disorder.

DEFINING BULIMIA

The term *bulimia* is from the Greek *bous limos* and means ox–hunger. Bulimia is characterized by episodes of compulsive overeating or binge–eating usually immediately followed (60% of the time) by self–induced vomiting to prevent weight gain from the overeating. Laxatives and diuretics are also used to prevent weight gain. Bulimics were once thought to have anorexia nervosa because many anorectics engage in some periodic binge–purge eating episodes; however, bulimia is now considered a separate disorder, although some bulimics develop anorexia nervosa. Psychiatrists once thought bulimia was a stage in the development of or an aftermath of anorexia nervosa, induced as a result of self–starvation.

A variation of bulimia, bulimarexia, has also been described. Marlene Boskind–White, quoted in *Bulimia: The Binge–Purge Compulsion* prefers to refer to binge–purging as bulimarexia and believes it is not a psychiatric disorder: "I don't even want to call bulimarexia an illness. We believe that bulimarexia is a habit. Like cigarette smoking and alcohol abuse, it may be a very serious habit, but still it's a habit. It has been learned, and it can be unlearned."

Janice M. Cauwels, author of *Bulimia: The Binge–Purge Compulsion*, believes the terms *bulimia* and *bulimarexia* shouldn't be used interchangeably, although the terms refer to the same gorge–purge behavior. The different therapeutic approaches—one viewing bulimia as a psychiatric disorder and the other viewing bulimarexia as a bad habit—suggest binge–vomiting behaviors may differ in degree of seriousness, and therefore treatment should vary accordingly.

In contrast to the anorectic, who revels in the sense of control she feels she has of her eating and the fear of loss of control, the bulimic is well aware of the loss of control of eating. Unlike the anorectic, she knows she has an eating disorder; she is obsessed with food and uses eating as an escape from the stresses of life. She is aware that her binge–eating goes beyond normal overeating and like alcoholics she makes periodic attempts to control her binges. About 20% of bulimics also abuse alcohol or drugs. The American Psychiatric Association recognized bulimia as a separate disorder in 1980 and described it as "consumption of a large amount of food . . . accompanied by an awareness that the eating pattern is abnormal, fear of not being able to stop eating voluntarily . . ."

Another contrast with anorectics is that most bulimics are either normal weight or overweight. It is thought about 10% of obese individuals occasionally binge–eat.

DIAGNOSING BULIMIA
Diagnostic Criteria

According to the *Diagnostic and Statistical Manual of Mental Disorders*, 3rd edition (DSM III) of the American Psychiatric Association, the diagnostic criteria for bulimia are:

A. Recurrent episodes of binge–eating (rapid consumption of a large amount of food in a discrete period of time, usually less than two hours)
B. At least three of the following:
(1) consumption of high–calorie, easily ingested food during a binge
(2) inconspicuous eating during a binge
(3) termination of such eating episodes by abdominal pain, sleep, social interruption or self–induced vomiting
(4) repeated attempts to lose weight by severely restrictive diets, self–induced vomiting or use of cathartics or diuretics
(5) frequent weight fluctuations greater than 10 pounds due to alternating binges and fasts
C. Awareness that the eating pattern is abnormal and fear of not being able to stop eating voluntarily
D. Depressed mood and self–deprecating thoughts following eating binges
E. The bulimic episodes are not due to anorexia nervosa or any known physical disorder.

Binge Eating Behavior

Most binge eaters are extremely secretive. Often close family members express complete surprise when they discover the bulimic's binge eating behavior. Some have binged for many years without ever being discovered by husbands, parents or children.

Binge eaters often engage in seemingly bizarre behavior to avoid detection; they usually have secure hiding places in which to binge, perhaps a closet. A locked bathroom is a favorite place, particularly if they plan to vomit after bingeing. Their food shopping sprees are sometimes similar to the obese overeater. They may buy food at several different stores in order not to arouse suspicion; they will chat with store clerks about "dinner parties" or "large family meals" to explain the large quantities of food they purchase. Bingeing can be very expensive, and so some binge eaters resort to shoplifting to help supply the large amounts of food—and sometimes drugs such as laxatives and diuretics—they require.

Binge eaters seem to prefer high–carbohydrate foods, foods that can be vomited up easily. Regardless of their normal table manners, most are messy eaters during their binges, stuffing food frantically into their mouths and gulping food, incompletely chewed. Some women prepare food especially for planned binges, cooking elaborate casseroles; others may go from store to store, eating their purchases immediately on the way to the next store; some may even binge in public, going from one restaurant to another.

Some binge eaters have specific times they set aside to binge—usually during a time they are least likely to be disturbed. Some have special foods they eat only on binges, foods they otherwise might feel are forbidden because they are fattening or non–nutritious. Some foods are selected because they "stuff down" easily and vomit up easily later. After a bingeing episode they may feel remorse and vow to themselves that the binge was the last time—much like an alcoholic after a heavy drinking bout.

The amount of food eaten in a binge can vary greatly; many binge eaters consume 10 times the food they would normally eat in a day. In *Eating Disorders: The Facts*, Suzanne Abraham and Derek Llewellyn–Jones report the food eaten by one patient during an eight-hour binge: three loaves of bread, five pounds of potatoes, one jar of honey, one jar of anchovies on bread, one pound rolled oats, two pounds pancakes, one pound macaroni, two instant puddings, four ounces nuts, two pounds sugar, one large packet of cereal, one and one-half pounds margarine, one pint oil, four pints powdered milk, one can condensed milk, four pounds ice cream, one pound sausage, one and one-half pounds onions, 12 eggs, one pound licorice, two family–size blocks of chocolate, one pound dried figs, two packets sweets, six health bars, assorted cream cakes eaten while shopping, one pound raisins, leftovers found in refrigerator and one bottle of orange cordial.

Researchers have estimated that as many as 75 to 90% of binge eaters take laxatives either during or after a binge, and some may take as many as 30 laxatives a day. As many as 40% of binge eaters may take diuretics instead of or as well as laxative.

WHO ARE THE BULIMICS?

Bulimics are obsessive–compulsive perfectionists, with high standards and low self–esteem. The profile of the bulimic is very similar to the anorectic in that it afflicts mostly young females. A 1981 study revealed that 19% of college women may have bulimic episodes; however, more recent studies released in 1988 are suggesting that the percentage of college–age women who have full–blown bulimia is actually much lower. Eating disorder specialists believe that most bulimics are not anorectic, and a minority of anorectics are bulimic.

Between 80 and 95% of bulimics are women. While some compulsive binge eaters experiment with vomiting and find they dislike it intensely, other binge eaters seem predisposed to binge–purge by vomiting.

Another category of people who may purge themselves are those who for professional reasons must maintain low body weight, although they are not necessarily bulimic and may or may not binge eat. They include dancers, actors, athletes and models.

CAUSES OF BULIMIA

Theories of bulimia's causes encompass both biological and psychological factors.

Biological Causes

According to *Consumer Research* magazine, "Many bulimics improve with antidepressant drugs, and most binges involve sugary foods. Both the drugs and foods promote serotonin synthesis in the brain, which results in an emotionally soothing effect." Serotonin, a neurotransmitter, is linked to both mood and eating functions, and decreased serotonin activity has been linked to compulsive behavior.

Another biological theory links a malfunctioning hypothalamus to all eating disorders, which causes a hormonal imbalance or inadequacy. However, it is thought more likely that the hormonal abnormalities are a result of malnutrition.

Psychological Causes

Although there is continuing research into the biological aspects of bulimia, it is largely regarded as being primarily an emotionally based illness in which the fear of food creates a compulsion that focuses reactions of stress and fear around episodes of binge eating. Dr. David Jimerson of the National Institute of Mental Health claims that seven out of 10 anorectics and bulimics are prone to depression, as are many of their relatives. Psychological studies have shown that most anorectics and bulimics have distorted attitudes and concepts that affect almost every aspect of their lives; for example, they tend to regard fat not simply as undesirable, but as disgusting, and they tend to regard any weight gain as evidence that their eating is out of control.

In some cases the onset of bulimia is thought to result from experimentation with isolated cases of vomiting to relieve an incidence of overeating and to prevent weight gain from the experience. The incipient bulimic then "discovers" purging as a method of weight control and the behavior escalates into full–fledged binge–purging in the same way smoking and drinking escalate into addictions. Doctors who accept this scenario feel that especially among young college–age girls self–induced vomiting is widely though intermittently used to prevent weight gain and that among those who do there is a percentage who are predisposed to full–fledged bulimia. In that regard its progression would be very similar to alcohol abuse.

Other events that may precipitate the first eating binge include domestic arguments, death in the family, school or job pressure, divorce or pregnancy.

PHYSICAL ASPECTS OF BULIMIA

Unlike anorectics, who are invariably emaciated, bulimics tend to be either normal weight or overweight. During binge eating some victims report that their feet and hands swell and some complain of nausea or abdominal pain, and by the end of the binge, headache and exhaustion.

About 60% of binge eaters induce vomiting at the end of the binge (and occasionally during the binge). Some become so adept at self–induced vomiting that they can begin vomiting just by constricting the muscles of the abdomen. Suzanne Abraham and Derek–Llewelyn Jones in *Eating Disorders: The Facts* report that

> some women use 'markers,' beginning a binge with food such as red apple skin, lettuce, or licorice which they can recognize in the vomit. A number of patients also use 'wash–out techniques': they keep on drinking water and regurgitating until there is no residue of food in their stomach, a process which can last up to half an hour. In most cases the vomiting episodes last from 5 to 30 minutes, depending on ease of vomiting and quantity. The women tend to exaggerate the amount of vomit describing the amounts regurgitated in terms of buckets full, ice–cream containers full, or saucepans full. To avoid detection they vomit into disposable containers or plastic bags. In one case the mother of the binge–eater habitually collected the vomited material and used it to fertilize the garden.

Prolonged bulimia causes vitamin deficiency and electrolyte imbalance that can trigger serious physical ailments such as liver, kidney and heart disease. Hair loss and bruising can also occur, and brain chemical changes can cause insomnia, depression and sometimes suicide. Vomiting can rupture the stomach, and the acid in vomit can erode tooth enamel.

About 40% of women with bulimia develop irregular menstruation, and about 20% cease menstruating altogether as in anorexia.

SOCIAL ASPECTS OF BULIMIA

Like the other eating disorders the incidence of bulimia is undoubtedly influenced by fashion pressures to be thin and the social fixation on the idea of thinness as beauty.

Bulimia has seemed to be on the increase, along with anorexia nervosa, and psychologists attribute at least some of the increase to the same social obsession with thinness that afflicts anorectics. Undoubtedly much of the apparent increase is also a result of the greater awareness of bulimia as more and more bulimics come out of the closet and seek treatment.

Singer Karen Carpenter, who died from emetine poisoning brought on by taking ipecac to induce vomiting, reportedly began her obsession to lose weight, which in turn brought on anorexia and bulimia, after reading a newspaper review of one of her performances that referred to her as "chubby."

Denise de Garmo, whose experience as a bulimic was turned into a TV movie called *Kate's Secret*, reports that she began her self–destructive behavior at age 19. Quoted in *People Weekly*, she said, "I was teaching exercise classes at the Sanctuary, *the* chic health club in Hollywood, where all the actresses went. One instructor had a great body and ate like a pig. I said, 'How do you do that?' She said, 'Easy. I throw up.' I thought, 'Great, this is painless.' " Her obsession became so severe that she became afraid to go to sleep, afraid that fat would form while she slept. Once she claims to have stayed awake for 10 weeks, weighing herself every hour and checking her body for formations of fat.

Many young professionals entering the treatment field have themselves experienced eating disorders, and it was their own recovery that prompted their interest in the profession. Tennie McCarty at Shades of Hope in Buffalo Gap, Texas is careful to refer to herself and to other former compulsive overeaters as "recovering" rather than "recovered." Because she believes that eating disorders are addictive in nature, like alcoholism and drug addiction, recovery is thought to be a lifelong process needing constant monitoring and peer support. Ms. McCarty also contends that treatment also reveals issues of childhood sexual abuse in the vast majority of women going through treatment, oftentimes so well repressed that clients claimed no conscious memories of the abuse until abuse issues surface during treatment.

"Sandy," a counselor at Shades of Hope, is a recovering bulimic. She claims to have been the "competent child" whose parents felt she needed no excessive nurturing, so competent was she at taking care of herself. Her family were Baptists and, like many similar families in West Texas, had religious and moral values which were both rigid and "somewhere just beyond attainment. Few children are able to live up to those religious expectations, and it's especially hard on the competent child, since an even greater degree of perfection is expected."

Sandy's childhood centered around pleasing her parents and her church. She was a youth leader, excelling in Sunday school and religious studies; she sang in the choir; and participated in all sports. Her rewards were Sunday family meals and the satisfaction that her siblings had reacted to the same family pressures and rigid values by "acting out" in the opposite direction. She entered treatment as a young adult when she realized that she was powerless over her food addiction.

TREATMENT OF BULIMIA

Unlike anorectics, who frequently need hospitalization at the beginning of treatment, bulimics are usually not in the same grave danger of death or serious incapacitation, and treatment is best begun outside the hospital. Exceptions are women whose lives are in crisis and need to be removed from their environment; however, in that event, a residential treatment facility will serve as well as a hospital.

A high rate of treatment failure has been reported. According to *Science News* in a study reported by Dr. David B. Herzog of the Massachusetts General Hospital in Boston, "After 18 months of treatment that included both psychotherapy and the use of antidepressant drugs, eight of 18 teenage bulimics were unimproved." Ten made significant improvements for about two months, then again developed symptoms of bulimia. "Four of 12 bulimic women in their 20s did not significantly improve for at least two months during the study. Some therapists are now suggesting that treatment with antidepressant drugs, once favored, is ineffective."

Other therapists are more hopeful about treatment outcomes. Janice M. Cauwels, author of *Bulimia: The Binge–Purge Compulsion*, writes that "pure bulimics seem to have the best chance for recovery as far as the eating itself is concerned. Rather than denying their problem, as do anorectics, bulimics are repulsed and frightened by their behavior. Once they have admitted to it, they don't resist treatment like anorectics—on the contrary, they feel an urgent need to get control of themselves. Having maintained normal weight and a more reasonable image of what their bodies look like, bulimics are more likely to develop normal eating patterns."

However, some bulimics refuse to cooperate, possibly because of underlying problems not touched by therapy. Dr. Elke D. Eckert, of the University of Minnesota, as reported by Cauwels, has proposed a theoretical model for anorexia and bulimia long–term treatment outcomes: "A normal–weight woman who develops anorexia may recover without becoming either overweight or bulimic. A restrictor anorectic [one who restricts food intake] can be treated and return to normal weight without developing bulimia; a bulimic anorectic, on the other hand, can return to normal weight and still have problems with bulimia. If the woman was overweight before becoming anorectic, she has a greater chance of becoming bulimic afterward; perhaps the bulimia was part of the obesity, since bulimics and obese people behave similarly. If she doesn't develop the complete bulimic syndrome, she may become overweight."

ANOREXIA NERVOSA AND BULIMIA IN MALES

The overwhelming majority of anorectics and bulimics are female, however about 15 to 20% are male. There is essentially no difference in the experiences of males and females with the disorders; whereas females experience either cessation of or erratic menstruation, males suffer reduced testicular function along with other advanced symptoms shared by females. Anorectic males tend to be obsessed with exercise and may be compulsive joggers. Male bulimics are much less well known because they are so secretive and because bulimics do not display the same obvious symptoms as do anorectics.

It was once thought that males were rarely troubled with distorted body image, one of the causes of anorexia nervosa and bulimia in women; however, researchers as reported in *Psychology Today* have found that many males as well as females are unhappy with their bodies. The researchers polled 226 college students about body shape and weight, as well as dieting and exercise. Forty–eight percent of the women and 26% of the men described themselves as overweight. Eighty–five percent of the women and 46% of the men wanted to lose weight. Forty percent of the men wanted to gain weight, and that percentage added to the percentage of men who wanted to lose weight indicates that about the same number of men as women are unhappy with their physical condition. The report did not state how many women wanted to gain weight.

Another difference between males and females was that women wanting to lose weight tended to diet and men tended to exercise to achieve weight goals. These researchers have speculated that "It may be that the key difference between the sexes with respect to the [development] of eating disorders is not dissatisfaction with body weight but rather actual behaviors related to diet and exercise . . . The chief risk factor for eating disorders may be dieting itself." The direction of many males' dissatisfaction with their bodies—wanting to gain as opposed to wanting to lose weight—may also be a factor in the large gender gap in the development of eating disorders.

OTHER EATING DISORDERS

PICA

Pica is a rare disorder usually afflicting retarded, neglected or unsupervised children and is characterized by the eating of nonfood substances such as clay, animal feces, paint, dirt, insects and pebbles. Children usually grow out of this habit as they grow older.

RUMINATION DISORDER OF INFANCY

After eating, infants with this rare disorder bring up their food for no apparent reason. They do not retch, but spit up food instead, sometimes chewing and reswallowing the food. This disorder can be fatal and may kill 25% of its victims, who die of starvation when not able to keep food down. When it occurs in adults, it is sometimes mistaken for bulimia.

PRADER–WILLI SYNDROME

Prader–Willi syndrome is a rare and little understood type of obesity characterized by a voracious and uncontrollable appetite. Victims are frequently retarded and in infancy are so limp they are unable to suck properly. Other characteristics sometimes include diabetes and underdeveloped genitals.

This disorder was first described in 1956 by two Swiss doctors, for whom it is named. There is no known treatment or cure.

TRENDS FOR THE FUTURE

A decade ago bulimia was unheard of outside the medical community. Anorexia nervosa was thought to be an exotic disorder better known for its mysterious contradictions for afflicting a few rich, privileged and beautiful women, none of whom would seem to have reasons for such relentlessly destructive behavior as self–starvation.

History and Treatment

Since widespread attention has begun to be focused on eating disorders two distinct trends have emerged: a tremendous amount of knowledge about the incidence, the causes and the treatment of anorexia nervosa and bulimia has developed; the other less positive trend has been an increase in reported cases of these disorders. In the case of bulimia, a large part of that increase has simply been bulimics who have secretly suffered alone without knowing they had a namable disorder; however, there is no question that both disorders were on the rise as the 1990s began.

The most hopeful sign for sufferers of eating disorders—apart from greatly advancing knowledge and ever–improving treatment techniques—is a new movement away from the social obsession with thinness. A growing number of books and articles, instead of focusing on the health benefits of weight loss, are concentrating on the well–being of the whole person, and the physical and psychological dangers of developing weight loss obsessions.

Within the past decade, increasing numbers of medical facilities, particularly at major medical schools and teaching hospitals, have opened eating disorders clinics, and many medical professionals are developing specialized knowledge about the field. A number of major, long–term studies are under way that will explore many of the mysteries still surrounding the subject of eating disorders. And perhaps, most hopefully, residential treatment facilities dedicated to treating the psychological dysfunctions underlying eating disorders are displacing, to some degree, the once–chic "fat farm" or weight loss spa, which concentrated solely on weight control, in many cases complicating the problem.

CHAPTER 2

CHRONOLOGY

1689

- Richard Morton is credited with the first description of anorexia nervosa in medical literature in his *Phthisiologia: or, a Treatise of Consumptions,* in which he describes Mr. Duke's 18–year–old daughter of St. Mary Axe, England as having "nervous atrophy," or *Atrophia vel Phthisis nervosa.*

1800s

- Low–carbohydrate diets are introduced for weight control.

1873

- The term *anorexia nervosa* is first used in England by physician Sir William Gull, who described the symptoms in several young upper–middle class English girls. In a speech in 1868 he described the symptoms of a "peculiar form of disease," which he then called "apepsia hysterica," later deciding "anorexia" was a more appropriate term.
- Charles Lasegue, a French neurologist, publishes a paper, "On Hysterical Anorexia," which details the symptoms of anorexia nervosa, which he refers to as a form of hysteria.

1900

- C. Von Noorden classifies obesity into two types: exogenous, due to overeating and underexercising; and endogenous, due to metabolism.

1920s

- Behavioral science pioneers Ivan Pavlov, Edward Thorndike and B.F. Skinner each begin important behavioral studies relating to eating responses.

1921

- Skinfold test to measure obesity is introduced, in which the thickness of a "pinched" fold of skin indicates the ratio of body fat to muscle tissue.

1929

- Invention of constant–tension calipers by R. Frazen improves accuracy of skinfold obesity test.

1932

- Premier Mussolini of Italy denounces dieting by women as harmful to the race.

1933

- Reducing drug called dinitro–ortho–creso is introduced by Drs. E.C. Dobbs and J.D. Robertson.

1935

- Surgeons in Budapest, Hungary remove 93 pounds of fat from 379–pound poultry dealer by making many small surgical incisions on his body.

1936

- Hormone Lipocaic, which controls utilization of fat, is discovered by Drs. L.R. Dragstedt, J. van Prohaska and H.P. Harms.

1943

- Boxer Joe Louis, at height of his athletic career, is deemed to be overweight by U.S. Army standards.

1947

- Dr. H.E. Richardson advocates treating non–glandular obesity in women as neurosis.

1948

- Scientists at Brown University link obesity to heredity.

Chronology

1950

- Dr. H. Millman reports on emotional factors in obesity.
- E.H. Rynearson reports on "emotional factors in overeating" and recommends formation of an organization to be called "Calories Anonymous."

1951

- Metropolitan Life Insurance Company starts drive to curb obesity and promote sound nutrition.
- Women on Long Island form "Fatties Anonymous," an organization similar to the later, more successful Overeaters Anonymous.

1953

- Dorset Foods begins marketing canned foods with calorie information printed on label.
- Knickerbocker Hospital in New York establishes obesity treatment center.

1954

- Dr. W.S. Kroger patents weight reducing belt that checks hunger pangs by pressing against upper part of stomach.
- Pituitary hormone adipoteinin is studied for its fat burning properties.
- J. Wolpe, in describing "avoidance conditioning" attempts to treat overeating with classical aversion methods using electric shock.

1956

- U.S. 12th Air Force in Europe orders overweight personnel to lose weight, and U.S. 18th Air Force in Greenville, S.C., puts senior officers on diet. A soldier is fined $110 and a sergeant is court–martialed for failure to lose weight.
- Connecticut textile worker, unable to do his job because of overweight, is ruled eligible for unemployment compensation.

1957

- Hilde Bruch postulates that obesity is consequence of personality defects in which body size becomes expressive of underlying psychological conflicts.
- U.S. House subcommittee holds hearings on misleading remedies for weight loss. Better Business Bureau says Americans spent $100 mil-

lion in 1956 on worthless remedies. The drug Phenyl propanolamine in reducing pills is declared harmful.

1959

- J.M. Strang reclassifies Von Noorden's metabolic obesity type, endogenous, to include breakdowns in the physiological or psychological regulation of food intake, and a type related to various endocrinological dysfunctions.
- First Metropolitan Life Insurance Company height and weight tables are published.
- In a criminal case in New York, the District Attorney calls Regimen brand reducing tablets fraudulent, raids office and seizes ads and television commercials. NBC drops company's TV commercials. Ads had shown models before and after weight loss and claimed weight loss was due to Regimen pills. Prosecution proved models had lost weight using other methods. Later in a criminal trial in 1965, the drug company, its ad agency and their executives are found guilty and fined: the ad agency is fined $50,000; the drug company president is given an 18–month prison sentence and fined $50,000; and the drug company is fined $53,000.
- Dr. Albert Stunkard and Mavis McLaren–Hume complete watershed analysis of obesity research, setting forth criteria for evaluating obesity research and reducing to eight the vast number of research studies that met criteria.

1960

- The Federal Trade Commission (FTC) charges Stauffer Labs with false claims of weight loss from "magic couch."
- Milk companies begin to market skim milk as diet food.
- Federal Drug Administration (FDA) seizes falsely labeled diet mixes.

1961

- Yale doctors find link between tendency to gain weight and heart problems.

1962

- Major study is published by U.S. Public Health Service (PHS) of weight, height and body dimensions of adults throughout the U.S.
- "Midtown Manhattan Study" directed by Dr. Lee Srole, establishes relation of obesity to social status, showing greater obesity in the lower socio–economic classes.

- W.L. Laurence reports new synthetic ACTH (pituitary hormone) compound that breaks down fat tissue into liquids.
- Reducing drug phenmetrazine (Preludin) causes deformities in newborns in Germany.

1963

- Aviation ministry in Great Britain grounds overweight pilots.
- Weight Watchers Society is founded by Long Island housewife Jean Nidetch.

1964

- French women discover "cellulite" and rush to spas and salons for treatment.

1965

- First intestinal bypass operation for weight loss is reported by American College of Surgeons.

1966

- M. Mendelson, in a pioneer study, delineates a continuum of the range of psychological disturbance in obesity causes.
- New York State appellate court upsets Regents Board's 1964 censure of Dr. Walter Sherman for negligence in treating obesity patients. Dr. Sherman, who specialized in treatment of obesity, overlooked conditions such as diabetes and prescribed amphetamine sulphate, desiccated whole thyroid and phenobarbital.
- New York civil court rules that Blue Cross must pay $557 hospital bill incurred in 1963 diet regimen administered in Mt. Sinai Hospital for Mrs. Jane Zorek. Blue Cross maintained that hospitalization was not necessary, but the judge ruled that "When multiple courses of treatment are available, whether for the obese, the alcoholic or the addicted, if the treating physician chooses that treatment for which hospitalization is required . . . absent a specific contractual exclusion, there is full coverage for the hospital stay."
- The U.S. Public Health Service (PHS) reports on obesity as a major health problem and finds diets are of limited value and urges exercise. The report rejects height and weight charts for tests for obesity and recommends skinfold pinch test instead.
- PHS publishes nationwide study of adult heights and weights and finds males are seven pounds and females 11 pounds heavier than found in the 1959 Metropolitan Life charts.

- New York state superior court awards Mrs. Elizabeth Ostopowitz $1,205,000 for injuries caused by taking anti–cholesterol drug Mer–29 to lose weight. The drug was withdrawn from the market in 1962 by its maker, the Richardson–Merrell Corporation, after its toxic effects were discovered. Mrs. Ostopowitz, who had Cushing's disease, suffered from cataracts, baldness and scaling skin, caused by the drug.
- Harvard University Public Health School study finds that colleges discriminate against obese in admissions.
- New York City Traffic Department dismisses several meter maids because they refuse to lose weight.
- NAAFA (National Association to Aid Fat Americans) is founded.
- Weight Watchers International company is founded. It is a spinoff of Weight Watchers Society founded in 1963.

1967

- Dr. Herman Taller, author of *Calories Don't Count*, is charged in federal court in Brooklyn with mail fraud and making false claims in promoting his book along with safflower oil diet pills marketed by Cove Vitamins and Pharmaceuticals. An ad company testifies that it lost the account because it refused to make strong claims without clinical evidence. Taller is convicted and fined $7,000; charges against the book's publisher, Simon & Schuster, and its ad agency are dropped.
- Professor A. Feinstein, on American Physicians College panel, asserts that being mildly obese poses no health risks.
- A New York City traffic department employee, J.M. Boutureira, who weighed 260 pounds and had been dismissed several times for being overweight, asks City Council to introduce resolution barring firing because of weight. City Council passes resolution.
- Scientists at Iowa University Medical College report that people who become obese, especially early in life, activate internal biological mechanisms that tend to keep them obese. The report hypothesizes an alternative pathway for disposing of excess glucose intake. Studies of obese children found that they produced low levels of the hormone dehydroepiandrosterone (DHA), which regulates the process of disposing of the excess glucose.
- At height of "be–in" era, 500 people hold "fat–in" in Central Park in New York to celebrate obesity.
- Senator Philip A. Hart's (Democrat, Michigan) subcommittee begins probe into diet pill industry, charging that manufacturers recruit doctors to promote drugs and also charges that obesity specialists use mass production procedures in treating patients.
- Dr. Alvan Feinstein at a meeting of the American College of Physi-

cians proposes that otherwise healthy, slightly obese persons not diet and cites harm of fad dieting. Dr. Jules Hirsch of Rockefeller University reiterates his contention on lack of scientific knowledge about obesity.

- Dr. Jean Mayer of Harvard reports on research to locate the seat of hunger and satiation signals in the brain. He describes the hypothalamus, a tiny region at the base of the brain. Studies show animals with an injured hypothalamus display confusion about hunger and satiation signals and consequently overeat.

1968

- *Weight Watchers* magazine is launched.
- Senator Philip A. Hart (Democrat, Michigan) subcommittee hearings produce evidence of indiscriminate dispensing of dangerous diet drugs containing thyroid extract, digitalis, amphetamines, barbiturates and prednisone at about 1,000 clinics across the U.S. Two companies, Western Research Labs and Lanpar Company, are charged. Lanpar Company president C.D. Brown testifies that company holds symposia at which doctors lecture on usefulness of products and that doctors were given discounts. Companies are ordered to cease marketing pills containing amphetamines and digitalis. In a related investigation, Illinois Narcotics Control Division probes death of nurse who died from amphetamine accumulation in her body after taking reducing pills.
- Dr. J. Hirsch of Rockefeller University claims that some persons with chronic obesity continue to "remember" and think of themselves as fat even after reducing.
- Hypnosis cure for obesity becomes briefly popular.
- J. Knittle, et al., conduct a series of studies showing that adipose cells remain constant throughout life and that by adulthood increases in body size are caused by increase in cell size, not cell number.

1969

- Drs. I.B. Perlstein, B.N. Premachandra and H.T. Blumenthal report to the American Therapeutic Society on study showing that some obese people produce antibodies against their own thyroid hormone, and gain weight because of the resulting metabolic imbalance.
- A study by R. Half Personnel Agency finds that higher–paid executives are thinner than lower–echelon employees.
- In a study on metabolism at Lankenau Hospital in Philadelphia it was found that the metabolic rate in a well-fed obese person and a starving lean person are similar because they both burn relatively more fat

and less blood sugar than normal persons, and it is thought that this is a vestige of early human behavior similar to some wild animals.

1970

February 8:   Two slightly overweight mothers, aged 24 and 27, in Monroe County, New York, are reported to have died after taking diet pills containing thyroid hormones, digitalis and amphetamines.

July 30:   National Research Council criticizes practice of limiting weight gain by pregnant women and recommends weight gains of 20–25 pounds during pregnancy, plus diet supplements.

August 6:   FDA proposes limiting the manufacture of amphetamines, an important ingredient in diet pills.

September 13:   Research report indicates overfeeding children produces excess of fat cells, which remain for life, hampering future weight loss.

November 17:   Drug industry promotions to doctors of reducing drugs is linked by the Narcotics and Dangerous Drugs Bureau of the U.S. Justice Department to increasing drug abuse.

1971

January 20:   Weight Watchers International, Inc. launches Operation HOPE in New York City to help people unable to leave home or function normally because of extreme obesity.

September 7:   Dr. J.L. Knittle, National Institute of Health researcher, finds that adult obesity can be predicted by age two because number of fat cells in body can be closely determined by that age.

September 12:   Weight loss fad Hot Pants, product name for inflatable shorts that allegedly reduces weight by increasing expenditure of energy, is investigated by the U.S. Postal Service. Test shows no weight loss by using the product.

October 12:   The Joffrey Ballet offers ballet classes as Think-Slim weight loss program for women.

1972

- Joseph Cautela introduces "covert conditioning" in treatment of obesity, which is based on "escape–avoidance" paradigm that punishes particular eating responses and reinforces responses antagonistic to eating.

August 4:   Skinny Liberation, group that feels society favors fat people is formed to focus attention on problems of thin people.

Chronology

September 28: The Better Business Bureau of Metropolitan New York mounts campaign against medical quackery relating to obesity control. It claims that Americans spend between $2 billion and $10 billion annually on useless gadgets and pills.

October 11: FDA reports on study it undertook to test claims of diet pills; study reveals that diet pills are no aid in weight reduction. It recommends imposing manufacturing quotas on amphetamines.

November 14: British study reports that babies born underweight suffer from educational and behavioral problems by the time they reach school age. Dr. N. Butler, director of the study, says effects were found in all social classes but most pronounced in lower socio–economic levels.

December 14: FDA moves to restrict harmful diet pills. FDA director E. Simmons mails bulletins to 600,000 health professionals warning of hazards of diet pills. In defending FDA's original action in permitting prescribing of diet pills for weight loss, Mr. Simmons said that a small number of people are able to lose weight taking the pills, and because the treatment of obesity is so difficult and includes high rates of failure, they believe that physicians should have use of all therapeutic aids.

December 14: In testimony before Senator Gaylord Nelson's (Democrat, Wisconsin) subcommittee Drs. Jean Mayer, J. Tepperman and T. E. Prout accuse the medical profession and drug companies of pandering to public misbeliefs about obesity and weight loss. Dr. Mayer cites diets such as "Drinking Man's Diet," rice diet, Mayo and Atkins diets as extreme and dangerous. Dr. Prout says that the American Medical Association (AMA) is abetting use of diet pills by failing to exert its influence to stop the practice and suggests that drug companies, which spend $12 million annually advertising in AMA publications, pressured AMA by persuading it to disband its Council of Drugs.

December 26: The $220-million salon and health spa industry is said to be permeated with fraud. Consumer agency investigators focus on deceptive ads, high pressure sales pitches and long–term contracts to attract customers. Health clubs run by Jack LaLanne and Nu–Dimensions are target of probe. Complaints include misleading ads, promise of improbable weight loss, dirty and overcrowded facilities and untrained instructors. Investigations reveal LaLanne's use of "future services" contracts, which customers are pressured to sign, requiring that they make all payments whether or not they actually use facilities. LaLanne claims that they do not enforce contracts; however, investigation of court records in New York City reveal that LaLanne spas sued more than 650 of its clients in 1972. New York State law specifies that for contracts worth over $500, signer is liable only for pro–rated time used plus 5% penalty.

1973

February 7: A federal grand jury in Newark, New Jersey, indicts G. Maisonet, E. Axel, D. Bradwell and V. Lynch for selling $1.1 million in phony diet pills by mail.

February 8: The Federal Office on Consumer Affairs warns against inflated claims and high pressure sales tactics used by spas and salons. The Federal Trade Commission (FTC) investigates sales tactics and claims of health clubs and spas; recommends limiting contracts to $500 rather than $1,000 and forbidding sellers to assign contracts to banks or others, and recommends triple damages to buyers who bring successful deceptive–practices suits.

March 9: AMA in warning against the book, *Dr. Atkins' Diet Revolution,* says the diets are unscientific and potentially dangerous; book recommends diet that activates fat–mobilizing hormone, converting stored fat to carbohydrates; advocates unlimited intake of fats and cholesterol–rich foods.

March 14: New York County Medical Society calls Atkins' diet unscientific, unbalanced and potentially dangerous to persons prone to kidney or heart disease and gout; it is called especially dangerous to pregnant women and unborn children. Dr. Atkins claims diets are based on clinical observation of 10,000 obese subjects over nine years.

March 21: U.S. District Judge F.B. Lacey asks postal service to begin probe of mail order sales of diet pills and upheld postal service's right to withhold mail delivery to Baslee Products Corporation of Bayonne, New Jersey which had been found guilty in nine counts of false advertising relating to sales of the diet pill Marvex.

March 22: Dr. Atkins, author of *Dr. Atkins' Diet Revolution,* is sued for $7.5 million in suit claiming his diet is responsible for heart attack as result of negligence and malpractice. Superior Court names Atkins, his associate I. Mason and publisher David McKay Company as co–defendants.

March 31: O.N. Miller, associate director of biological research for Hoffman–La Roche, granted patent for obesity control product using nicotinic acid to inhibit growth of fatty substances known as lipids. Hoffman–La Roche is testing product on animals.

April 2: FDA and Bureau of Narcotics and Dangerous Drugs recall diet drugs containing amphetamines. Action includes injectable amphetamines and closely related chemicals and all combination diet pills that contain amphetamines and other ingredients such as sedatives or vitamins. It is the largest recall of controlled drugs to that date. The action meets strong opposition from drug companies and doctors. Injectable drugs banned include dextroamphetamine, levamphetamine and meth-amphetamine. Amphetamines are also used to treat narcolepsy and some psychiatric or behavioral problems.

April 7: New Jersey Assemblymen A. Imperiale, W. Foran and J. Bornheimer sponsor a resolution honoring tenth anniversary of Weight Watchers Society; month of June is declared Weight Watchers Month. Weight Watchers International founder J. Nidetch honored at Madison Square Garden in New York with Bob Hope, Pearl Bailey, Roberta Peters and Ruth Buzzi.

April 9: New York City Consumer Affairs Department passes regulation prohibiting noncancellable contracts for "future service" aimed especially at reducing salons and spas.

June 7: American Chemical Society in a study conducted at Loyola University's Stritch School of Medicine in Maywood, Illinois reports on fat–reducing agent FMS (fat–mobilizing substance) found in urine of those who are fasting. It is thought to play a role in rapid breakdown of fat during starvation. FMS appears to stimulate the release of a form of adenosine monophosphate known as cyclic–AMP, which promotes the enzyme lipase that breaks down fats. The chemical structure of FMS is unknown, but it is thought to be a protein.

June 14: Bureau of Narcotics of the Justice Department places restrictions of prescription nonamphetamine diet pills which include ingredients such as benzphetamine, fenfluramine and phendimetrazine, and are sold under many trade names as appetite suppressants. Illicit drug world begins underground sales in an effort to replace lost sales because of unavailability of amphetamines. Most of restricted drugs have been placed in Schedule 3 of the Federal Controlled Substances Act, which requires everyone handling drugs to register and requires manufacturers and wholesalers to maintain safeguards to prevent theft and to prevent prescription refills of more than five times in a six–month period. Trade names of some drugs affected are Voranil, Sanorex, Pondamin, Tenuate and Tepanil.

August 7: E. Axel pleads guilty of conspiring to commit mail fraud in the sales of $1.1 million in diet pills advertised as Slim–Tabs 33 slenderizing tablets and admits to being principal of Stanford Research Corp., arranging "fronts" as corporate officers, and receiving $50,000. D. Bradwell also pleaded guilty and receives two–year suspended sentence and three years probation.

Eating Disorders

August 21: Cassette tape recording designed to help in weight loss is marketed by Accomplishment Dynamics Company and narrated by Dr. R.E. Parrish, who says tape uses technique similar to hypnosis.

September 22: D.R. Salata receives patent for Rollslim, massaging device consisting of two rollers, for overweight women.

October 19: Liberty Life Insurance Company announces hospitalization program with premium rates based on insured's weight; overweight persons will pay higher premiums.

October 21: A Brooklyn College study involving mice finds that overweight mice live only half as long as normal–weight mice, and many of the overweight develop diabetes, become sluggish, inactive and almost sterile, and have low sex drive; process is reversed by reducing mice's weight. Professor G.H. Fired says experiment corroborates accepted theories about proper exercise and nutrition. Study is based on more than 1,000 mice over 10–year period.

October 27: L. Avedon, formerly Princess Pignatelli, with J. Moli introduce their diet book, *The Beautiful People's Diet Book*, which describes diets of several "beautiful people."

November 11: National nutritional study of more than 20,000 Canadians finds more than half the population are overweight and attributes cause to sedentary lifestyle rather than overeating.

November 26: Drug Guild Distributors, manufacturer of X–11 Reducing Plan Tablets, agrees to discontinue misleading and harmful advertising. Tablets are considered by medical authorities as potentially harmful to those suffering from heart disease, high blood pressure, diabetes or thyroid disease, despite ad statement that they are safe for everyone. Company agrees to full refund to customers who are dissatisfied but admits no violation of law.

December 27: Dr. J. Hirsch and J. Knittle and colleagues report on people who have been fat since childhood and have larger than normal number of fat cells and claim that the earlier in life obesity begins, the larger the number of fat cells.

December 27: Dr. Jean Mayer says persons of particular body type— slender ectomorphs with long, narrow hands and feet—are unlikely to become fat; other researchers note that infant feeding practices lead to overfeeding, which in turn creates a greater number of fat cells. Researchers found that mothers of fat children tend to respond to their infants' distress by feeding; later these children react to emotional stress or frustration by eating.

Chronology

1974

January 23: Operator of weight reducing products company, Raymond Carapella, pleads guilty to mail fraud in multi–million dollar per year sales of diet pills and bust–developing products.

May 6: FTC begins New York regional investigation of sales of future service contracts by reducing salons.

June 15: Brewster Produce, a mail order house, admits in federal court in Newark, New Jersey, that it sold almost $2 million worth of phony diet pills.

July 17: FTC accuses Jack LaLanne health spas of deceptive practices in membership pricing; company agrees to cease and desist without admitting law violation.

August 31: Patent is issued for mirror device that shows how obese person will look after considerable weight loss.

September 15: Woman on fast weight loss diet dies of heart attack after fasting for four days.

September 16: Several weight loss clinics are the subject of federal investigation into fraudulent practices for falsely advertising medical supervision and using unapproved drugs. Chain–operated clinics charge fees of $175 to $500 for 21– to 40–day treatment consisting of low calorie diet and daily injections of hormone HCG (human chorionic gonadotropin) obtained from urine of pregnant women, which clinics admit may be worthless, but they justify its use on psychological grounds; FDA bans interstate shipment of HCG.

November 10: Citing studies showing anorexia nervosa as having a fatality rate higher than any other psychiatric disorder, the Philadelphia Child Guidance Clinic claims 100% cure rate for children who remain in treatment.

December 12: U.S. postal service bars mailing of fraudulent products Slimmer Shake and Joe Weider's Weight Loss Formula XR–7 made by Weider Distributors Inc. of Norwood, New Jersey.

December 15: FDA announces that drugs containing hormone HCG must be labeled as worthless for weight loss.

1975

March 27: Jack Fried, operator of Phase Method, is indicted in Newark, New Jersey on mail fraud charges for selling weight reduction plans based on clients' handwriting samples. Fried is latter convicted and sentenced to three years in prison.

April 4: Pillsbury Company announces it will acquire Weight Watchers International Inc. for $43 million.

May 14: Slim–Tabs Slenderizing Tablets producer Arnold Mandell pleads guilty to mail fraud, admitting pills are worthless.

August 18: Joseph Marano, owner of Body Beautiful Inc., consents to New York State superior court judgment closing weight reducing company.

August 22: FDA recalls Enrico Caruso Pure Corn Oil, manufactured by Caruso Products Distributing Corporation, for falsely labeling the product "slenderizing" and showing a picture of a young woman.

August 26: 21st Century Communications, publisher of *Weight Watchers* magazine, announces that the magazine will be taken over by *Family Health* magazine.

December 15: Federal Trade Commission (FTC) prohibits Stuart Frost Inc. from advertising body wrapping devices called Slim–Quick or services used for weight reducing.

1976

March 3: Americans for Democratic Action issue a report attacking the weight reducing industry, citing $90 million annually wasted by consumers.

March 26: A study is published showing that early puberty and menstruation of girls is associated with stoutness and late menstruation with thinness.

June 9: FTC Judge Daniel H. Hanscom rules that Porter & Dietsch Inc., makers of X–11 Diet Tablets, and its ad agency, Kelly Ketting Furth, falsely advertised that users could lose weight while eating as much as they wanted.

December 4: Two government employees patent a method of controlling obesity with purified "miracle fruit" grown in West Africa.

1977

March 12: Because of saccharin's role in causing cancer, FDA announces plans to classify saccharin as a drug instead of a food additive. Diabetes organizations respond that unavailability of saccharin could lead to an increase in sugar use and resulting increase in diabetes, heart disease and arthritis.

April 5: Dr. R. Lee Clark, president of the American Cancer Society, says that diabetes and obesity pose more immediate dangers to Americans than possibility of cancer caused by saccharin.

Chronology

April 11: Dr. John E. Farley, Jr., head of the Rhode Island Medical Society drug abuse commission, announces his organization's opposition to the use of amphetamines in treating obesity; Utah Medical Association also opposes amphetamine use.

May 19: At an FDA public hearing on saccharin sales–curb proposal, opponents of the curb stress benefits of saccharin in weight control; Dr. Sidney Wolfe, director of Health Research Group, counters saying saccharin is not necessary in weight control.

June 21: In the first major malpractice suit under a new Pennsylvania law, Marlene Baumiller, who underwent intestinal bypass operation for weight loss, is awarded $100,000 from Dr. Robert Cassella, who accidentally punctured her spleen and had to remove it; $25,000 from Pittsburgh Podiatry Hospital; and $225,000 from Medical Professional Liability Catastrophe Loss Fund.

July 21: FDA proposes strict rules for labeling foods as low calorie.

August 29: At annual American Psychological Association meeting Dr. Judith Rodin says overweight people secrete more insulin when stimulated by food sights and smells. Increased insulin secretion increases hunger, leading to overeating.

August 30: In a report in *Pharmaceutical Sciences Journal,* Dr. Sarfaraz Niazi claims weight is lost when liquid perfluoroctyl bromide is used to coat gastrointestinal tract, temporarily blocking food absorption; Dr. Theodore B. Van Itallie voices skepticism.

September 20: In Porter County (Indiana) superior court Cora Staniger is awarded $50,000 in damages from doctors who put her on a protein deficient diet during her pregnancy, causing mental retardation of her daughter.

October 24: The Oklahoma chapter of the American Civil Liberties Union (ACLU) charges that Oral Roberts University is violating federal law regarding equal treatment for handicapped in general and fat people in particular in requiring that all students 10% overweight enroll in "pounds–off" program.

November 3: FDA and Center for Disease Control (CDC) begin inquiry into 12 deaths suspected to be caused by liquid protein diet formula, which supplies 300 calories per day in a liquid made of fibrous protein collagen from animal tissue. Investigators suspect it may deprive users of potassium. FDA names a panel to investigate.

November 24: Federal Disease Control Center reports 10 more deaths suspected tied to crash dieting with predigested liquid proteins. FDA Commissioner Donald Kennedy requests 35 manufacturers of product to label compounds as hazardous under some conditions. Senator Charles Percy urges FDA to reclassify these diet products as prescription drugs.

November 27: In testimony before the FTC the Kellogg Company says charges that its ready–to–eat cereals contribute to obesity are "hysterical allegations."

December 1: At an American Heart Association meeting, California heart specialists claim that liquid protein diets can result in death even if used under strict medical supervision.

December 21: Figures from National Health Statistics Center show that American adults weigh an average of about four pounds more than in the previous decade.

December 29: At a House Subcommittee on Health and Environment hearing about liquid protein diets Dr. Robert Linn, author of *The Last Chance Diet*, questions the accuracy of the government report linking the diet to deaths.

1978

January 27: FDA asks 800,000 professional health workers to report cases of liquid protein–caused health problems; 46 deaths and 200 injuries from product are to be investigated. Sales of the product plummet.

February 12: Luciano Pavarotti, having lost 90 pounds on diet, disproves myth that obesity helps opera singers project strong voices.

March 12: Fat Liberation Front announces drive to free fat people from stigma and claims that no health problems result from obesity. Dr. Robert Sherwin of Yale comments that organizations such as the Fat Liberation Front help the obese psychologically but warns that obesity still needs to be treated.

April 22: Dr. Feridun Gundy of Queens, New York is convicted in federal court of illegally dispensing $2.5 million worth of amphetamines to obese patients.

May 16: Dr. George Blackburn, whose research was partially the basis for liquid protein diets, warns that the diets dangerously deplete essential nutrients.

May 16: H.J. Heinz Company announces that it will acquire Weight Watchers International Inc. for over $71 million.

July 22: Calorie counter to be worn on wrist is invented.

September 22: Statistics are cited by Bruce Hannon and Timothy Lohman of the University of Illinois showing that if all overweight people in

America dieted to normal weight, one–time energy savings would be equivalent to 1.3 billion gallons of gasoline.

September 22: Drs. Arthur Hartz and Alfred Timm, and mathematician Eldred Geifer announces that research at the Medical College of Wisconsin shows that environment is more important than heredity in determining tendency to obesity, disputing previous studies showing heredity as more important. Study observed behavior among natural and adopted siblings with overweight mothers, who were selected from weight reduction organization TOPS (Take Off Pounds Sensibly).

October 15: Substantial decline in sales of liquid protein diets is reported; decline is attributed to FDA findings of deaths by users of products. All deaths reported were of women who all died of myocarditis, inflammation of heart tissue. Government says because of drastic drop in sales, banning product is less urgent.

December 17: Survey by British shirt manufacturer shows that fewer than 20% of women are attracted to skinny men, while 34% prefer men to have "slight suggestion of a paunch and 31 percent like a bit more of a paunch."

December 30: FDA revises order for warning labels on liquid protein diets and now requires warning on all protein products that provide more than 50% of a person's calories and are promoted for weight loss or as a food supplement.

1979

February 20: New research study challenges heredity–caused theories on obesity; the new study shows overeating as primary cause.

April 24: Weight Watchers International introduces new exercise plan, Pepstep, that concentrates on walking to aid in weight loss.

May 13: FDA panel headed by Dr. John W. Norcross reports that phenylpropanolamine and benzocaine, found in several nonprescription diet aids, may help some dieters; calls for further study on other ingredients; and reports that dozens of others are worthless.

July 1: FDA requirements for strict labeling of diet foods goes into effect. Foods labeled "low calorie" are required to contain no more than 40 calories per serving and must be lower in calories than food normally found in grocery stores. Foods labeled "reduced calorie" must contain at least one–third fewer calories than similar products for which it is substituted. Comparisons must be shown on label.

July 17: FDA proposes crackdown on illegal amphetamine use by banning their use in weight reduction. FDA says ban would reduce pill production by 80 to 90%. Three and one–third million prescriptions for amphetamines were written in 1978.

August 10: In an ongoing trial, New York State Appellate division refuses to dismiss a $30 million libel suit brought by Great Neck Dr. Joseph Greenberg against CBS TV program "60 Minutes." In a program interview Barbara Goldstein told how Dr. Greenberg allegedly gave her amphetamines for weight reduction, claiming he had ordered her to take as many as 80 pills per day. Mike Wallace and producer Grace Diekhaus are named co–defendants. Court says elementary standards of news reporting may not have been met because Greenberg was not properly questioned by "60 Minutes" on the truth of the allegation. The suit is later settled out of court.

August 25: Greek government releases film shorts and other educational material urging Greeks to stop overeating. In Greece, where people are 12 to 16 pounds heavier than Americans and other Europeans, obesity is traditionally associated with good health.

December 15: A study is reported in medical journal *Lancet* claiming that bypass surgery is safe and quick way to loose weight. *Lancet* editorial questions validity of study, criticizing research design and calling project ethically unsound.

1980

February 10: Essex County, New Jersey chapter of NOW (National Organization for Women) sponsors program called Food, Fat and Feminism, which explores reactions to fat and fat people, and food and diet.

March 8: Electronic calorie counter, called Cal–Count, that displays number of calories being burned while both asleep and awake, is patented.

March 16: Marlene Viveiros, who is five feet, one inch and weighs 210 pounds, files discrimination complaint with Providence, Rhode Island, Human Relations Commission against Homemaker Health Aid Services of Rhode Island, who she claims dismissed her because of her weight.

April 6: After the murder of Dr. Herman Tarnower, co–author of the *Scarsdale Diet*, his book jumps from third to first place on *The New York Times* mass–market paperback best–seller list.

May 1: Five drug companies agree to FDA request to stop shipments of new nonprescription diet products containing twice the current legal limits of phenylpropanolamine hydrochloride (PPA), an appetite suppressant drug. FDA determines that recalls are not necessary because pills are not considered a health risk.

May 4: A study is reported that finds that although death rates are higher for people who are above average weight, death rates are higher still for those weighing less than average.

May 29: A report by the Food and Nutrition Board of the National Academy of Sciences says healthy Americans need not worry about fat and cholesterol and admits its stand dissents from other major organizations that urge curbs on fat and cholesterol. Government experts criticize the report, saying board members ignored important scientific data.

July 5: Diet preparation that suppresses appetite for calories but not proteins is patented by Richard J. Wurtman, Judith J. Wurtman and John D. Fernstrom, and licensed for production by Massachusetts Institute of Technology.

September 28: Research linking stress to obesity is reported. Rats reportedly overate when their tails were pinched, but their appetites abated when given naloxone, an opiate antagonist. This research has implications for understanding stress–related overeating.

October 30: A study is reported showing evidence that obese people have a biochemical defect involving enzyme adenosine triphosphatase (ATPase), which helps pump sodium and potassium across the membranes of body cells. ATPase may be responsible for 10 to 50% of the body's heat energy production. The amount of ATPase in the red cells of the obese group was 22% lower than in the nonobese in the study.

December 12: A study by Drs. Eugene Lowenkopf and L.M. Vincent finds that 15% of students in professional ballet schools suffer from anorexia nervosa and many others are borderline. The study attributes dancer's obsession with body weight to the ballet profession's emphasis on thinness.

1981

January 4: Weight Watchers International reports licensing of first weight loss spa, located in Santa Rosa, California.

January 9: A study is published in *Science* magazine that challenges popular belief that high–protein, low–carbohydrate diet is best way to lose weight.

January 26: Dr. Richard Proctor, founder of Elaine Powers Figure Salons, Inc., announces a high–nutrition meal replacement formula called Sensible Eating Formula, to be sold through Elaine Powers salons.

June 22: Ed Koch, mayor of New York City, after failing to lose weight on diet, announces plans to take appetite suppressant pills.

August 4: New York State passes law making amphetamine prescription for sole purpose of weight loss illegal.

August 11: Study by Drs. Linda Craighead, Albert Stunkard and Richard M. O'Brien finds that appetite suppressant drugs may be counterproductive to long–term weight loss.

October 31: Psychotherapists report that bulimia nearly always begins with stringent weight loss diet.

November 16: An *AMA Journal* report criticizes the book, *The Beverly Hills Diet*, saying it is filled with medical inaccuracies.

1982

February 13: A report is published saying 10,000 poisoning cases per year result from taking PPA (phenylpropanolamine).

March 9: Study by Richard Weindruch and Roy L. Walford finds that undernutrition begun in middle age can lead to longer and healthier life for mice.

July 2: FDA announces that starch blockers, sold as diet aids, are possibly dangerous drugs and must be removed from market. Bio–Tech Laboratories, manufacturer of the pills, sues FDA to prevent defining starch blockers as drug.

August 22: Federal judge in Chicago denies request by FDA for ban on starch blockers despite a report of 75 illnesses related to the pills.

August 24: American Dietetic Association announces it will publish *Food/2* magazine, first published by the U.S. Agriculture Department during the Carter administration, which is based on federal dietary guidelines that deal with weight control and with modified fat and cholesterol diet.

October 10: Federal court classifies starch blocker diet aids as drugs and ends all sales until determination of their safety can be made.

October 24: Gastroplasty, new operation that seals off most of stomach, is reported.

November 22: Suction lipectomy, new surgery that removes body fat by suction, is reported.

1983

March 2: Metropolitan Life Insurance Company publishes new height and weight tables showing ideal weights have increased for men by two to 13 pounds and three to 8 pounds for women.

April 28: Dr. Edward R. Woodward warns of life–threatening side effects resulting from jejunoileal bypass, a surgical procedure to lose weight by bypassing small intestine.

July 5: Cornell University study finds exercise after eating is the best way to get rid of extra calories and finds exercise crucial in maintaining stable weight when daily caloric intake fluctuates.

July 23: Dr. Thomas R. Knapp of the University of Rochester recommends people abandon concept of "ideal weight" because it is based on inconsistent data.

1984

January 23: A growing obesity problem is reported in India as more urban dwellers move into the middle class. Previous attitudes that overweight signified respectability are being rejected as weight loss centers proliferate.

February 23: An opinion poll finds that 72% of Democrats and 56% of Republicans believe politicians should lose weight.

December 16: A new eating disorders program is reported at Phelps Memorial Hospital in North Tarrytown, New York that treats anorexic and bulimic patients who require extensive care.

December 16: Pump therapy for anorexic patients is reported to pump up to 2,000 calories a day into severely underweight patients.

December 21: A Study at Massachusetts General Hospital by Dr. Nancy A. Rigotti finds that women with anorexia nervosa often have weak bones, but can be treated with exercise.

1985

February 14: A National Institutes of Health panel defines obesity as a disease and says it should receive the same medical attention as high blood pressure, smoking and other factors that cause serious illness and premature death, and that overweight should be treated when it reaches 20% above "desirable" weight.

March 19: A study reported in *Journal of Abnormal Psychology* finds that women have negatively distorted view of their bodies; men also have distorted image of their bodies, but it is more positive.

March 22: Physicians and psychotherapists specializing in anorexia nervosa and bulimia treatment ask FDA to ban over–the–counter sales of syrup of ipecac, a drug used to induce vomiting, because of its potential use by bulimics.

May 6: A study by Dr. William Dietz, of the New England Medical Center, and Dr. Steven Gortmaker, of the Harvard School of Public Health, finds that children who watch lots of television exercise less, eat more and become obese.

August 6: Dr. Reubin Andres challenges Metropolitan Life height and weight tables, saying weight ranges given in tables do not reflect ideal weights.

September 2: First free–standing residential facility in U.S. devoted exclusively to treatment of anorexia nervosa and bulimia, Renfrew Center in Philadelphia, is reported.

1986

May 22: Scientists report that anorexia nervosa sufferers have high levels of cortisone, hormone excreted by adrenals in response to fear.

1987

March 24: Dr. George Blackburn, obesity specialist at Harvard Medical School, comments on study on causes of obesity and finds that dieting is ineffective for many people because when they reduce food intake, their metabolic rate drops to protect them from starvation.

1988

January 17: Federal researchers report that Americans' weight averages seem to vary state by state.

February 11: A study by Dr. William Feldman of Ottawa University reports that girls come to believe thin is beautiful as early as age seven and links that attitude to rising incidence of eating disorders in young girls.

February 25: Two studies are published showing evidence of genetic causes of obesity: one study was of Pima Indians in Arizona, the other of infants in Britain. These studies confirm theories of Dr. Jules Hirsch of Rockefeller University, who has promoted the idea for over two decades.

March 22: Doctors specializing in bulimia report that use of antidepressant drugs can help some patients reduce binge eating and purging, but warn that they cannot replace psychotherapy needed to get to the root problems.

April 17: Wilkins Center for Eating Disorders in Greenwich, Connecticut survey says among anorectics and bulimics, number of those who are 12 years old or younger has doubled in the last two years from 3 to 7% and says rise indicates increasing social pressure for thinness.

1989

January 3: Researchers at Rockefeller University announce discovery that abnormally low levels of protein adispin, which is secreted directly into the bloodstream by fat cells, may be linked to tendency to gain weight when not enough adispin is secreted. It may be a factor in genetic tendency to obesity.

February 23: A University of Michigan study is released that finds American women aged 18 to 34 have been getting fatter over past several decades; black and poor women and women with low education levels show the greatest weight gains.

March 18: Ronald T. Stunko patents chemical method of preventing fat formation in humans.

July 1: Pharmacologist Mark Hohenwarter patents biamine, chemical for treating addictions such as food or cocaine. Biamine works by replenishing certain neurotransmitters in the brain.

September 16: Cardiologists Jackie R. See and William E. Shell patent "Fat Magnets" diet pills, made from bovine bile, that prevents the body from absorbing some fat and cholesterol in food.

October 3: Merck Sharp & Dohme announce discovery of manner in which hormone cholecytokinin triggers brain to tell body when to stop eating. They also discovered two chemicals that block hormone's action.

November 26: Calorie Control Council announce survey that indicates 48 million Americans were on diets last year, a 26% decline from 1986. The same survey claimed that 96 million Americans regularly consume low calorie foods and beverages, up 19% from 1986.

December 12: Centers for Disease Control releases a study that finds that Hispanic Americans, on average, tend to be more overweight than other Americans.

1990

January 3: Nationwide survey by Calorie Control Council finds that pounds almost always return after dieting and that only fundamental changes in eating behavior will keep them off. Survey also found a 26% drop in the number of people on diets.

March 20: Research team led by David Williamson of the Federal Centers for Disease Control announces findings that people are most likely to gain weight as young adults and that black women are especially vulnerable; women of all races are twice as likely as men to gain large amounts of weight; and women from 25 to 44 who were overweight at the beginning of the study gained the most weight of all subjects.

March 28: Representative Ron Wyden (D., Ore.) chairman of the House Regulation, Business Opportunities and Energy subcommittee opened hearings into questionable practices of the weight-loss industry amid charges that health risks, false advertising and profiteering are "bedrock" in the industry.

April 1: Five-year study by Dr. Thomas Wadden shows that 98 percent of all dieters regain their weight within five years.

April 1: *New York Times* story says recent studies suggest that formula diets can lead to psychological and physiological burdens that limit diets' long-term effectiveness; some people develop fear of food and become dependent on formula diets, while others binge and suffer humiliating weight gains, while few maintain their lower weights.

CHAPTER 3

LEGAL ISSUES RELATING TO EATING DISORDERS

INTRODUCTION

Most court cases relating to eating disorders are concerned either with issues of discrimination based on an individual's condition resulting from the eating disorders or on issues of eating disorders as a handicap or disability, and often involve disability pension benefits or rights to educational, medical or job benefits under the Federal Rehabilitation Act of 1973. There have also been cases that established the obligation for insurance companies to reimburse the treatment of eating disorders.

Eating disorders are frequently cited as contributing to and being symptomatic of other underlying disorders, and therefore don't become issues in themselves. For example, obesity is frequently cited as a contributing factor in many instances of disability caused by diabetes, high blood pressure and some heart conditions.

In addition there have been numerous criminal prosecutions for fraud in the diet and weight loss industry. Although legally the frauds do not differ from any other type of fraud, which usually relate to deceptive sales and advertising practices, the weight loss industry has become a fertile field for those seeking quick riches through touting of weight loss gimmicks and schemes, mostly because the uncertainty about causes and treatment makes prosecution difficult. Despite the large number of prosecutions, questionable treatment for eating disorders, particularly obesity, continues.

DISCRIMINATION ISSUES

In 1974 Catherine McDermott was offered a job at the Xerox Corporation, subject to passing the company's routine physical examination. Ms. McDermott was five foot six inches and weighed 249 pounds. The examining physician found her medically unacceptable because of her obesity and the job offer was withdrawn.

Ms. McDermott sued and the case reached the New York court of appeals. She was awarded $1,000 for mental anguish and humiliation, plus back pay and a position at Xerox. The New York Human Rights Law prohibits employers from refusing to employ persons with disabilities that are unrelated to job performance.

Xerox based its defense on the statistical likelihood that obesity would cause future medical problems for Ms. McDermott and would additionally affect Xerox's disability and life insurance rates.

The court agreed that Ms. McDermott's obesity constituted an impairment but did not find that it would interfere with her job performance.

In another employment case, in 1979 United Airlines fired flight attendant Ingrid Fee for being overweight. Ms. Fee, who at five feet seven inches, weighed 143 pounds, which was four pounds over the weight limit in the company's job description. United Airlines used the Metropolitan height and weight charts as the criteria for weight limits for its flight personnel. Ms. Fee hired a lawyer and was subsequently reinstated.

INSURANCE AND DISABILITY ISSUES

In a 1966 case involving insurance reimbursement for hospital treatment, New York civil court ordered Blue Cross to pay a $557 hospital bill incurred in 1963 by Mrs. Jane Zorek when she was hospitalized in Mt. Sinai Hospital for treatment of obesity. Blue Cross maintained that hospitalization was not necessary, but the judge ruled that "When multiple courses of treatment are available, whether for the obese, the alcoholic or the addicted, if the treating physician chooses that treatment for which hospitalization is required . . . absent a specific contractual exclusion, there is full coverage for the hospital stay."

Another case in New York State involved the obligation of the state to provide appropriate education services for the handicapped, or alternatively to pay providers for the services. Lara Antkowiak was an adolescent suffering from anorexia nervosa and a profound emotional disturbance which surfaced when she was about 10, several years after the death of her mother. According to her father, John Antkowiak, M.D.,

76

Lara did not show any indication of emotional difficulty after her mother's death and progressed academically and socially. In 1983 at age 10, Lara became increasingly anxious about schoolwork and began to withdraw from her family and friends and began spending all her play time doing homework. In 1983 her doctor noted that she had gained no weight during the past year and placed her in Strong Memorial Hospital in Rochester, New York. Lara had been hospitalized several times, once for nearly a year. During her hospitalization at Strong her schooling was continued by doing homework packets from her school. She then returned to school briefly, but was readmitted to Strong in 1984, this time to the psychiatric unit, where she deteriorated and was transferred to a medical unit. During that hospitalization, Lara was tutored by a special education teacher at Strong. The tutor testified in the later court case that at first Lara was cooperative and responsive; however, she eventually regressed, and by mid–April of 1985 refused to come to class. A psychologist who subsequently examined Lara "found her to be one of the most disturbed children I had seen in my practice . . ."

Dr. Antkowiak, Lara's father, was advised to look for a program that could deal with Lara's emotional, educational and social needs as well as her physical problems. Unable to find a facility in New York State that would accept Lara, Dr. Antkowiak sent Lara to the Devereaux Foundation in Eastern Pennsylvania and applied to New York State Education Department (SED) for funding for Lara's placement under the federal Education of the Handicapped Act (EHA) and the Rehabilitation Act. The Buffalo Committee on the Handicapped (COH) supported the application, stating that six New York State institutions had rejected Lara. The Education Department rejected the application on the grounds that the out–of–state facility was not approved for use by New York State residents. Dr. Antkowiak sued the Department of Education for tuition reimbursement, which was about $4,000 per month.

Dr. Antkowiak contended that Lara was entitled to appropriate treatment and education at the expense of the New York State Education Department under the provisions of the Education for the Handicapped ACT (EHA) and the Rehabilitation Act. The Education for the Handicapped Act requires states receiving federal funds under the act to ensure that all children in need of special education and related services are identified and provided appropriate programs. The State Education Department had initially resisted the contention that Lara's anorexia was, in fact, a handicap. After examination, the state relented, but insisted that Lara be placed in a New York State facility and rejected the Devereaux Foundation placement on the grounds that it was not on the list of approved out–of–state facilities.

Judge Curtin of the United States District Court, Western Division, New York, in ordering Lara's placement at the Devereaux facility found that SED, the defendant, was required by EHA to provide Lara a free, appropriate education. He also found that the defendant did not dispute the suitability of Lara's placement at the Devereaux Foundation, nor had the defendant come up with any alternate appropriate approved facility.

In ordering reimbursement for Lara's father, it was further found that education authorities may be required to reimburse parents fully for privately placing their children in treatment facilities if it can be determined that the placement was proper under terms of the EHA.

The court's decision provides parents of any handicapped child, not only a child with anorexia, with new legal clout in intervening on their children's behalf when education authorities breech their duties either by neglecting to recognize the severity of the handicap, as the SED did initially in Lara's case, or in neglecting the child through bureaucratic wrangling, as the SED did in Lara's case by erecting legalistic barriers to finding an acceptable facility for Lara. While the court did not find that Lara's father could skip the requirement to exhaust administrative solutions before bringing suit, it did seem to recognize that in dealing with children at an age when the child passes from one developmental stage to another, it is not possible to take time out of the development process to sort out legal issues relating to the child's education as it would be possible in adult cases which might be litigated for years without causing any developmental harm. In other words, in cases such as Lara's, events must be dealt with as they occur rather than as directed by administrative needs of the SED. That means that parents can take an active and aggressive role in holding education authorities accountable to the terms of EHA.

CONSUMER FRAUD ISSUES

Because dieting and weight loss is a multibillion–dollar industry, the temptation for companies and individuals to participate in consumer fraud is enormous. Moreover, because the state of scientific knowledge relating to issues of obesity and weight loss are often contradictory and frequently suppositious and unconfirmed, the temptation for even well–meaning physicians and others to stretch the interpretation of appropriate weight loss treatment to its outer limits in order to generate enormous profits is obviously overwhelming, as evidenced by the large number of companies, doctors and other professionals who have been accused or convicted of bilking the public with fraudulent or questionable weight loss schemes. Some examples out of many include the following:

In 1965 a private company, New Drug Institute, pleaded guilty in federal court in Brooklyn, New York to conspiring to produce false clinical reports exaggerating the effectiveness of a diet drug called Regimen. As a result of using the falsified reports in advertising, the drug maker defrauded the public of millions of dollars. In a related case government prosecutors charged the maker of the drug, Drug Research Corp., with false advertising by portraying before and after pictures of models, purporting to show dramatic weight loss. Noted nutritionist Jean Mayer, as an expert government witness, demonstrated that the models in the company's ads could not have lost the weight claimed in the time claimed, using the drug. An executive at the company's ad agency, Kastor, Hilton, Chesley, Clifford and Atherton, which prepared the ad, admitted that the agency knew the advertising was false. The drug company, the testing lab and the ad agency were fined.

Just two years after the Regimen case, the well–known case of Dr. Herman Taller was tried. In 1960 Dr. Taller had published *Calories Don't Count*, a book that became a best–seller. Part of Dr. Taller's diet recommended taking capsules of safflower oil to speed weight loss, and he endorsed the maker of the pills. The prosecutor in federal court in Brooklyn pointed out in his charge against Taller that Simon & Schuster, the book's publisher, had arranged a promotional link between the book and safflower oil capsules marketed by Cove Vitamins and Pharmaceuticals. As a result, Taller was convicted of mail fraud, conspiracy and food and drug rules violations and fined for making unsubstantiated claims for the capsules in order to promote their sale. Complaints against Simon & Schuster and its ad agency were dropped.

Since these cases were tried, dozens of companies, doctors and other individuals have been similarly prosecuted for making false advertising claims, mail fraud and violating FDA regulations regarding the use of drugs, but because the potential for profit is so great, the relatively small fines are not sufficient to even slow the practice, much less stop it. In addition, not every case of suspected weight loss fraud is prosecuted or even investigated. For every case that results in fines, jail terms or business closures, many more operations continue business on the margins of the law, unscathed.

CHAPTER 4

BIOGRAPHIES

Arcuni, Orestes Admitting psychiatrist at Payne Whitney Clinic, New York Hospital. Dr. Arcuni and his colleagues at Payne Whitney run one of the foremost pioneering treatment programs for eating disorders.

Arenson, Gloria Director of Eating Disorders Treatment Center in Los Angeles. A former binge eater, she has developed workshop programs that help short-circuit binging behavior—both in the long term and on an emergency basis. Her philosophy stresses that by dealing with underlying problems, compulsive eating behavior can be brought under control.

Atrens, Dale Professor of psychology at the University of Sydney and an Australian TV personality. He argues on TV and in his book *Don't Diet* that the dangers of being overweight are overstated and possibly less debilitating than the dangers of dieting, which he contends can lead to eating disorders.

Bockar, Joyce Psychiatrist. One of the few dieters who have successfully maintained weight loss, she has successfully treated other obese individuals and wrote about it in her book *The Last Best Diet Book*.

Brody, Jane Nutrition columnist for the *New York Times*. She writes often about eating disorders, particularly anorexia nervosa and bulimia, and frequently reports on new treatments and studies in the field.

Bruch, Hilde Psychiatrist. Born in Germany, Hilde Bruch taught for more than 20 years at Baylor Medical School until her death in 1984. She is widely regarded by professionals researching and treating eating disorders as the originator of modern-day eating-disorder treatment practices. Her book *The Golden Cage*, published in 1978, is cited by almost every major author writing about anorexia as providing the basis for understanding the psychological aspects of anorexia.

Byron, George Gordon   Late 18th-, early 19th-century poet. Frequently thought to be an ideal of male beauty, the young Byron was obese. He later achieved and maintained his thin adult physique by dieting and self-starvation, a program he followed for life. At age 19, he was five feet eight and a half inches tall and weighed 202 pounds. He chewed tobacco and smoked cigars to help suppress his hunger.

Carpenter, Karen   Singer. A member of the singing siblings The Carpenters, she died after becoming anorectic and bulimic, reportedly after reading a review that called her "chubby," focusing her attention on her physical appearance and thus beginning her eight-year obsession with her weight. Her story was portrayed in a 1988 CBS TV movie, *The Karen Carpenter Story*.

Dublin, Louis I.   Zoologist. In his long career at Metropolitan Life Insurance Company, he was responsible for many innovative programs promoting the health of policyholders. It was Dublin who popularized the idea, through many articles in scientific journals and popular magazines, that being overweight caused poor health. It was his study on which the original Metropolitan Life height and weight tables were based.

Elliott, Cass   Singer, member of the rock group The Mamas and Papas. Overweight, Mama Cass, as she was known to her fans, went on a crash diet and lost 100 pounds. She died of complications caused by rapid weight loss.

Emmett, Steven Wiley   Unitarian-Universalist minister and psychotherapist. In his psychotherapy practice he specializes in eating disorders and is director of the Anorexia Nervosa Aid Society of Rhode Island and clinical consultant for the Renfrew Center in Philadelphia, the nation's first freestanding institution devoted solely to the treatment of anorectics and bulimics.

Fabrey, William J.   Founder of the National Association to Aid Fat Americans (NAAFA). He is not obese himself, but his wife weighs more than 200 pounds. He founded the organization in response to the frustration his wife and other obese friends experienced dealing with overt discrimination and to provide mutual support in developing self-esteem among obese people.

Fallon, Patricia   Psychologist. In her practice in Seattle she specializes in the treatment of bulimia. She conducts workshops, participates in research and writes on the subject.

Friedrich, William N.   Faculty member of the Mayo Clinic in Rochester, Minnesota, he is a consultant in the department of psychiatry and psychology, where he is active in both family therapy training and family treatment. He is the author of over 50 journal articles and book chapters.

Garmo, Denise de   Author of the story portrayed in the TV movie *Kate's Secret*, about a woman with bulimia and anorexia nervosa. The movie is based on de Garmo's experience. She began her binge-purging behavior after her marriage at age 24, attributing much of her problem to the pressures she felt as the wife of a high-powered entertainment lawyer.

Greene, Herbert   Broadway conductor. Herbert Greene was once vastly overweight, but he successfully overcame a food addiction and compulsive eating habits. In doing so, he developed his own method for maintaining control, which he shares in a book called *Diary of a Food Addict* that he wrote with his wife, actress Carolyn Jones.

Gregory, Dick   Comedian. He has branched into the nutrition and weight loss business, marketing a product called Slim-Safe Bahamian Diet, a weight-loss powder. It is marketed primarily through ads in black publications. He recently bought a hotel in Alabama, which he is turning into a nutrition and weight-loss center.

Gull, Sir William   Nineteenth-century English physician. Gull was the first to name anorexia nervosa. As court physician to Queen Victoria, he observed the puzzling disorder among young privileged women.

Hauser, Gayelord   Natural scientist, writer, lecturer and teacher. In the 1940s and 1950s he had a large following of devoted readers and students for his brand of healthful living. He helped popularize the use of natural food and the idea of correct eating as the key to good health. Some of his ideas are once again gaining popularity, this time among professional health workers.

Hirsch, Jules   Professor at Rockefeller University. Dr. Hirsch is one of the most respected authorities on the problems of obesity; he has directed research studying obesity in both animals and humans. He is past chairman of the National Institutes of Health panel on obesity and past president of the American Society of Clinical Nutrition. Dr. Hirsch is a leading proponent of biochemical causes of obesity, as opposed to primarily psychological reasons.

Hudson, Walter   World's heaviest man. Although he has now lost nearly 400 pounds after more than a year of dieting, he once weighed 1,200 pounds and was so heavy he was unable to get out of bed.

Kempner, Walter   Physician, originator of the rice diet. He was a refugee from Nazi Germany who devised the famous "rice diet" in the 1940s for patients with hypertension. The diet, which consisted of unsalted rice, fruit and fruit juice, later attracted people who used it primarily for weight loss and who visited Dr. Kempner's Durham, North Carolina clinic in large numbers for many years.

Keys, Ancel   Researcher. He was responsible for the first and largest study of the effects of starvation. During World War II, 36 conscientious objectors volunteered to spend 24 weeks on a starvation diet in an effort to develop methods to rehabilitate starved populations in war zones. This research and other Keys' studies are still widely cited.

Lasegue, Charles   Nineteenth-century French neurologist. In a paper published in 1873 called *On Hysterical Anorexia*, he described the cycle of the condition later recognized as anorexia nervosa as a struggle for control between a teenage female victim and her family, each using food as a manipulative weapon. He contended that it was usually a "real or imagined marriage proposal" that triggered the condition, advantageous marriage being the Victorian middle-class goal for that society's young girls. The symptoms of anorexia became the girl's weapon for regaining control of her life.

Levenkron, Steven   Psychotherapist and author of *The Best Little Girl in the World*. He adapted the kangaroo pump for use in treating anorexia nervosa. The pump was originally developed for feeding patients after stomach surgery. It pumps as much as 2,000 calories a day into anorexia patients and helps accelerate weight gain.

Mannix, Jeffrey   Author and counselor. He established the Mannix Clinic for Behavior Training and Control, which deals largely with behavior modification to control overeating. He also is a consultant for the Institute for Studies of Destructive Behaviors, the Suicide Prevention Center, several major corporations, sports teams and government agencies. He has written a book explaining his method, called *The Mannix Method*.

Mayer, Jean   Nutritionist. Born in France and highly decorated during World War II, Dr. Mayer studied both at Yale and at the Sorbonne in Paris. Now president of Tufts University, he taught at Harvard for many years. Also for many years he wrote a newspaper column about nutrition, the problems of weight and eating, and related matters. In addition he has written numerous books and articles, both scholarly and popular, and has been involved in much of the important research relating to eating and eating disorders. He is considered one of the foremost experts in the field of nutrition and eating disorders.

Miller, Estelle   Psychotherapist and founder of the American Anorexia Nervosa Association. In addition to her duties running the association, she lectures about anorexia nervosa and conducts group therapy sessions for victims.

Biographies

Millman, Marcia   Sociologist. She conducted in-depth studies of overweight and obese women and the problems they faced because of their handicaps and how they responded. Dr. Millman turned her research into a best-selling book, *Such a Pretty Face.*

Nidetch, Jean   Business executive. She founded Weight Watchers in 1963 after reducing from 213 to 142 pounds with the help of a high-protein diet developed by Norman Jolliffe of the New York City Department of Health. She has been a consultant to the New York State Assembly Mental Hygiene Committee and an adviser to the (New York) Joint Legislative Committee on Child Care Needs. She has written several books, including *The Story of Weight Watchers* and two cookbooks.

Orbach, Susie   Feminist. Her book *Fat is a Feminist Issue* infuriated many fat women by claiming that many women become fat in order to get men to take them seriously as people rather than sex symbols.

O'Neill, Cherry Boone   Daughter of singer Pat Boone. Cherry O'Neill wrote a first-person account of her struggle with anorexia nervosa in her book *Starving for Attention.* She tells what it is like living a fishbowl celebrity existence and the pressure to be perfect, which sometimes leads to eating disorders, particularly anorexia.

Patton, Sharon Greene   Author of *Stop Dieting—Start Living!.* Sharon Greene Patton published one of the earliest accounts of dieting failure that seriously questioned the medical wisdom of weight loss through dieting. She contended that her health improved once she stopped dieting.

Polivy, Janet   Professor of psychology and psychiatry at the University of Toronto. She is among the growing number of antidiet psychologists and physicians who claim that dieting itself can lead to eating binges when people are too long deprived of foods that they really want or need. She advocates self-acceptance rather than weight loss as the key to change.

Pritikin, Nathan   Diet-book author and early advocate of a low-cholesterol diet. Once a controversial figure because he was self-taught and lacked academic credentials, he developed a low-fat, low-cholesterol and whole-grain diet to combat disease and obesity. He founded the Pritikin Longevity Center in Santa Barbara, California in 1976, and before his death in 1984 he was guardedly accepted by much of the medical community.

Russell, Lillian   Late 19th-, early 20th-century actress. She is often cited as proof that plump, voluptuous women were once considered beautiful, as indeed she was. Famous for her "hour-glass" figure, she was tall, and at her maximum weighed more than 200 pounds.

Simmons, Richard   TV host. Formerly overweight, he parlayed his successful weight loss into a successful TV weight-loss show and a book, *Never Say Diet*.

Root, Maria P.P.   Clinical psychologist. She is a nationally recognized expert in the treatment of eating disorders and has a private practice in Seattle. She teaches at the University of Washington, consults, conducts workshops, researches and writes about eating disorders.

Rowland, Cynthia   TV journalist. A bulimia victim herself, she suffered in secret for 12 years before seeking help. She is now executive director of the Bulimia Association of America, lectures on the dangers of bulimia and has written about her struggle with bulimia in her book *The Monster Within*.

Schachter, Stanley   Social psychologist. He conducted several well-known experiments in the 1960s that tested the relationship of internal body signals to obesity. He found that fat people seemed to ignore bodily signals altogether, a finding that seemed to undercut the popular theory that obesity results from inner conflicts.

Stoler, Shirley   Obese actress. She was perhaps the first obese actress to play dramatic roles rather than comedy. Beginning with *The Honeymoon Killers* in 1970, in which she starred, she has proved that her large size can add to the dramatic impact of her performances.

Stunkard, Albert   Professor of psychiatry, University of Pennsylvania. He has directed or participated in much of the important research relating to eating disorders and now argues in favor of a physiological cause for obesity and the body weight "set-point," which keeps weight constant. He is a favorite of reporters seeking expert commentary on new or trendy eating disorder treatments and diets as well as new scientific discoveries related to the field.

Subby, Robert C.   Addiction expert. The contribution of co-dependency of family members to alcohol addiction has been recognized for several years. However, it is only recently that co-dependency has been recognized as a factor in many instances of eating disorders. Mr. Subby has written about co-dependency as well as worked with co-dependents. He is a founding board member of the National Association of Children of Alcoholics, executive director of Family Systems Center, and program director of the Life Design Out-patient Chemical Dependency and Compulsivity Treatment Program in Minneapolis.

Van Itallie, Theodore B.   Formerly co-director of the Obesity Research Center at St. Luke's–Roosevelt Hospital Center in Manhattan. Dr. Van Itallie has been an outspoken critic of prepared diet formulas that provide 400 to 800 calories per day in the form of a liquid or powder. His concern is that rapid weight reduction causes loss of lean body mass at a greater rate than loss of fat, putting a strain on the heart muscle.

Wooley, Susan and Wayne   Directors of the Clinic for Eating Disorders at the University of Cincinnati Medical College, they have been pioneers in advocating the "non-dieting approach" to controlling eating disorders. They believe that fatness is largely biologically determined, and one of their main goals is for women to change their own views of their obesity, thereby liberating themselves from self-imposed guilt about their weight.

PART II

GUIDE TO FURTHER RESEARCH

GLOSSARY

Actuarial: *adj.,* in the insurance industry, refers to statistics of death or accident claim rates, which determine the degree of risk for issuing insurance policies.

Addiction: a habit or dependency, usually bad, extremely difficult to overcome, sometimes because of chemical reactions caused by drugs in the body, but also said of some psychological dependencies such as overeating.

Adipose cells: fat cells.

Amenorrhea: interruption or cessation of the menstrual cycle for any reason other than pregnancy or menopause.

Amphetamine: *alpha–methyl–phenyl–ethyl–amine* ($C_9H_{13}N$), a drug formerly prescribed as an appetite suppressant in treatment of weight loss; now highly restricted because of side effects and dangers of addiction. Sold illegally in the drug underground, and commonly called "speed."

Angina pectoris: a heart condition characterized by a sharp, sudden pain of short duration in the chest, relieved by nitroglycerin.

Anorectic: *n.,* one suffering from anorexia nervosa; also the adjective form of anorexia.

Anorexia nervosa: extreme emaciation caused by a refusal to eat, usually as the result of gross misperception of one's body as being overweight.

Anthropologist: a scientist who studies the social, physical and cultural development of mankind, including customs and beliefs.

Anxiety: a state of tension or fear resulting from anticipation or uncertainty, or sometimes having no apparent cause.

Arrhythmia: a heart condition characterized by an irregular heartbeat; loss of rhythm.

Arteriosclerosis: a loss of elasticity and narrowing of the passages of the arteries caused by deposits of plaque; commonly called "hardening of the arteries."

Bariatric medicine: a branch of medicine treating problems of overweight and obesity.

Basal metabolism: in physiology, the energy required to maintain the body's essential functions at rest, measured by oxygen intake and heat discharge.

Behavior modification: in psychology, a process of changing habits by applying external stimuli such as rewarding desired activity and punishing undesired activity.

Binge: for people with eating disorders, an episode of uncontrollable eating in which large quantities of food are consumed.

Bingeing and purging: an episode in which binge eating is followed by vomiting.

Borderline syndrome: a psychological condition in which individuals are unable to relate to or love others.

Bulimarexia: a condition resembling bulimia and characterized by bingeing and purging, but in a milder form.

Bulimia: an eating disorder characterized by binge eating followed usually by self–induced vomiting, a syndrome which the victim is unable to control.

Bulimic: *n.,* one who suffers from bulimia, also the adjective form of bulimia.

Carbohydrate: in nutrition and dietetics, foods such as sugars, starches and cellulose; its chemical composition is carbon combined with hydrogen and oxygen.

Cardiovascular: *adj.,* pertaining to the heart and blood vessels.

Cathartic: a laxative.

Cirrhosis of the liver: a disease of the liver, characterized by a breakdown of cells.

Co–dependency: in psychology, refers to symbiotic relationships in which a family member reinforces disordered behavior of another member. Co–dependents are often said to be "addicted to relationships" and lose self–identity through overidentifying with the problems, usually alcohol, drug or food addictions, of a spouse or other family member.

Compulsion: an irresistible impulse to perform an act, beyond the control of the actor.

Compulsive eating: uncontrollable binge eating.

Cosmetic surgeon: in medicine, a surgeon who performs operations primarily to change the look of the body rather than because of a medical disorder.

Dehydration: in physiology, a condition in which the body fluids are dangerously depleted.

Demographic: pertaining to demography, the study of population statistics such as size and distribution.

Glossary

Densimeter: instrument for measuring specific gravity of a substance.

Depression: in psychology, a state of extreme dejection characterized by withdrawal, low energy and unresponsiveness to stimulation.

Diabetes: a condition associated with insufficient insulin production by the body, causing excessive sugar in the blood and urine.

Dietitian: one who practices dietetics, the science of diet and dieting. See also Nutritionist.

Diuretic: a drug or other substance that eliminates excess water in the body by increasing urine production.

Eating disorder: maladjusted eating patterns or distorted responses to food because of underlying psychological problems. The three major eating disorders are obesity, anorexia nervosa and bulimia.

Edema: an excess of fluid collected in body tissues and organs, usually causing swelling.

Electrolyte: a fluid solution that conducts electricity; in the human body, ionized salts in the blood.

Emaciation: a state of extremely low body weight relative to height, usually characterized by having a body weight less than 20% of the ideal as defined by the Metropolitan height and weight charts and usually caused by disease or an eating disorder.

Emetine: white alkaloid powder obtained from ipecac and used to induce vomiting.

Energy: the capacity for doing work; in the body, results from the metabolism of nutrients.

Epidermis: the outer layer of the skin covering the body.

Fat: *n.,* one of the substances in body cells consisting of fatty acids and glycerol; *adj.,* referring to one who is overweight or obese.

Feeding tube: a device used in hospitals to assist patients who cannot swallow or sometimes used to force–feed anorectics who have difficulty eating.

Fiber: the filaments of plant and animal tissue; essential in the human diet to provide bulk.

Genetic: *adj.,* pertaining to inherited characteristics in plants and animals.

Glucose: a chemically simple form of sugar, a monosaccharide carbohydrate ($C_6H_{12}O_6$), and used for intravenous feeding.

Gout: a condition caused by excessive uric acid in the bloodstream and characterized by swelling and pain in the joints, especially the big toes; a form of hereditary arthritis.

Heart attack: a malfunction of the heart muscle caused by an occlusion (closure) of one of the coronary arteries.

Hibernation: a state of dormancy in which some animals pass the winter. Metabolism slows to a very low point so the animal can survive on stored fat, obviating the need for food.

Hormone: substances produced by the endocrine glands and used in specific body functions such as growth, metabolism, menstruation, etc.; for example, insulin is a hormone essential in the metabolism of sugar.

Hunter–gatherers: in anthropology, people who lived before the advent of agriculture by hunting animals and harvesting wild plants.

Hydrometer: an instrument for measuring the density or specific gravity of a liquid.

Hyperalimentation: feeding technique used in hospitals in which patients are fed complete nutrition intravenously.

Hyperinsulinemia: a condition in which insulin levels in the body are higher than normal.

Hypertension: high blood pressure.

Hypothalamus: a gland that regulates various body functions such as temperature and some metabolic processes.

Hysteria: an old–fashioned medical and psychological term describing frenzied emotional states in women.

Insomnia: the inability to sleep.

Insulin: a hormone secreted by the pancreas and essential in the metabolism of sugar. Injections of insulin are given to diabetics, whose bodies produce insufficient insulin.

Intravenous feeding: a technique used mostly in hospitals in which nutrients, mainly glucose, are given directly into the patient's vein through a tube from a bottle or plastic pouch suspended above the patient's bed.

Ipecac: an emetic, used to induce vomiting when suspected poisonous substances have been eaten; an essential drug in an emergency medical kit.

Kangaroo pump: a device developed to feed people after certain surgical procedures that make swallowing difficult; it has been adapted for the feeding of anorectics who refuse to eat.

Lanugo: soft down hair covering the body.

Laxative: a drug taken to relieve constipation.

Liposuction: see **Suction lipectomy.**

Menses: See **Menstruation.**

Menstruation: in women's fertility cycle, a monthly period during which blood flows from the uterus.

Metabolism: the process by which food is converted and burned in the body, creating energy.

Glossary

Neurotransmitter: a chemical that transmits nerve impulses.

Nutrition: a process converting food into body tissue; as generally used in discussing diet and health, the health–giving properties of food.

Nutritionist: a health professional specializing in the field of nutrition; a scientist researching the field. See also **Dietitian.**

Obese maturity onset diabetes: a form of diabetes that strikes in adulthood; it is characterized by an excess of or normal amount of insulin produced by the body, and in that way is the opposite of juvenile onset diabetes.

Obesity: an excess of body weight above the norm, usually at least 20% above the weights listed in the Metropolitan height and weight charts.

Overweight: an excess of weight above the norm, but less severe than obesity.

Pedometer: a device used to measure distance when walking.

Physiological: *adj.,* pertaining to physiology.

Physiology: the study of processes and mechanisms of living organisms.

Pica: a rare eating disorder of childhood characterized by the eating of nonfood substances.

Pinch test: see **Skinfold test.**

Pituitary gland: the gland at the base of the brain that secretes hormones affecting growth and metabolism.

Prader–Willi syndrome: a rare eating disorder characterized by voracious appetite.

Protein: a component of plant and animal tissue made up of combinations of amino acids; an important component of animal muscle tissue.

Psychological: *adj.,* pertaining to any aspect of the human or animal mental processes.

Puberty: the point at which sexual maturity occurs and reproduction becomes possible; signaled in girls by the onset of menstruation, which can occur anytime between ages 10 and 16; signaled in boys by the enlargement of the testicles and the beginning of pubic hair growth, usually between the ages of 11 and 15.

Purge: see **Bingeing and purging.**

Rumination disorder of infancy: a rare eating disorder in which infants spit up food without vomiting.

Schizophrenia: an aberrant mental state affecting thinking, mood and behavior, usually characterized by delusions, withdrawal or conflicting emotions.

Schizophrenic: one who suffers from schizophrenia.

Sedentary: *adj.*, sluggish or inactive.

Serotonin: a chemical in the body thought to be important in sleep and sensory perception.

Skinfold test: a test that determines the percentage of body fat by measuring a pinched fold of skin, using special calipers.

Stress: emotional strain or pressure, usually resulting from conflict, overactivity or other form of overstimulation.

Subcutaneous layer: the layer of flesh just beneath the skin's outer covering.

Suction lipectomy: a surgical procedure for removing body fat in which suction instruments are inserted into the subcutaneous layer and fat cells are sucked from the body.

Syndrome: a group or set of symptoms, which in combination indicate the presence of a disease or condition.

Thermogenesis: the production of heat, especially in the body.

Uric acid: a substance in urine ($C_5H_4N_4O_3$), which when crystallized, forms the basis for kidney stones; also a factor in gout.

Varicose veins: veins that have been abnormally distended, principally in the legs.

Vitamin: substances found in minute portions in food that perform special physiological tasks in the maintenance of tissue; essential for normal metabolism, growth and development.

ACRONYMS AND INITIALS

AA	Alcoholics Anonymous
AABA	American Anorexia/Bulimia Association
ANAD	National Association of Anorexia Nervosa and Associated Disorders
ANRED	Anorexia Nervosa and Related Eating Disorders
ASBP	American Society of Bariatric Physicians
AY	Abundantly Yours
BBI	Buxom Belles International
CDC	Centers for Disease Control
CHS	Community Health Services
COH	Committee on the Handicapped
FDA	Federal Drug Administration
LL	Lean Line
MEDLARS	Medical Literature Analysis and Retrieval System
NAAFA	National Association to Aid Fat Americans
NAAS	National Anorexic Aid Society
NCHS	National Center for Health Statistics
NHPIC	National Health Planning Information Center
NIH	National Institutes of Health
OA	Overeaters Anonymous
PHS	Public Health Service
SED	State Education Department
TOPS	Take Off Pounds Sensibly

GOVERNMENT PROGRAMS

There are no special programs or major government initiatives for dealing with eating disorders. However, the federal government is involved in several indirect ways. Eating disorders research receives major government support. The FDA is involved policing treatment programs that generate millions of dollars from Americans wanting to overcome eating disorders, especially obesity. Some of the government agencies involved in various aspects of eating disorders are:

COMMUNITY HEALTH SERVICES (CHS):
This agency distributes literature and sponsors community–based information programs. Contact: Community Health Services, Public Health Service, Department of Health and Human Services, 5600 Fishers Lane, Room 7–05, Rockville, MD 20857; phone 301–443–2320.

FEDERAL DRUG ADMINISTRATION (FDA):
The FDA provides information on all drugs used in the United States. In addition it is the agency that polices drug use in the treatment of obesity and other disorders. The FDA publishes and distributes more than 200 free publications, many relevant to nutrition and eating disorders such as those on vitamins, minerals and drug regulations. A free catalog can be ordered from the Office of Public Affairs, Food and Drug Administration, Department of Health and Human Services, 5000 Fishers Lane, Rockville, MD 20857; phone 301–443–3210.

NATIONAL HEALTH PLANNING INFORMATION CENTER (NHPIC):
This agency performs free data base searches for health professionals needing bibliographic and abstract information regarding all aspects of health care including eating disorders. The Clearinghouse on Health Indexes provides statistical and other information on topics in all health fields. The Health Information Clearing House provides a useful referral service for almost any question concerning any aspect of health and can be contacted at 1555 Wilson Blvd., Suite 600, Rosslyn, VA 22209; phone 703–522–2590.

NATIONAL INSTITUTES OF HEALTH (NIH):

This agency has sponsored symposia on eating disorders and has funded research through its Clinical Nutrition Research Units, a cooperative program of the National Cancer Institute and the National Institute on Aging, the National Institute of Arthritis, Diabetes, and Digestive and Kidney Diseases.

The NIH publishes an almanac covering its activities and can be obtained from Editorial Operations Branch, Division of Public Information, NIH, Department of Health and Human Services, Building 31, Room 2B03, Bethesda, MD 20205; phone 301–496–4143.

NATIONAL LIBRARY OF MEDICINE:

This is the largest research library in a single scientific field and provides information on many topics relating to eating disorders from its collection of three million books, journals, technical reports, and audio–visual materials. Any library can request material from this facility through interlibrary loan. The library can also perform computer searches of its data base, called MEDLARS (Medical Literature Analysis and Retrieval System). Contact: National Library of Medicine, NIH, Department of Health and Human Services, Rockville, MD 20209; phone 301–496–6095.

ORGANIZATIONS

ABUNDANTLY YOURS (AY)
P.O. Box 151263
San Diego, CA 92115
(619) 697–9862
Abundantly Yours was founded in 1979 by Joyce L. Rue, who is also its director. Its motto is "being the best you are regardless of size," and its purpose is to educate and enlighten both fat people and the general public and to remove stigmas associated with being fat. It sponsors theater and camping trips and organizes self–help workshops aimed at fostering emotional, physical and psychological well–being. It also provides referrals for special needs of fat people, bestows awards, operates a speakers' bureau and placement service and compiles statistics.

AMERICAN ANOREXIA/BULIMIA ASSOCIATION (AABA)
133 Cedar Lane
Teaneck, NJ 07666
(201) 836–1800
AABA was founded in 1978 as the American Anorexia Nervosa Aid Society by Estelle Miller. Its members are anorectics, bulimics, parents of anorectics and bulimics, psychiatric social workers, nurses, psychiatrists and physicians. The association offers counseling and organizes self–help groups. It maintains a speakers' bureau and collects research information. It publishes a newsletter.

AMERICAN SOCIETY OF BARIATRIC PHYSICIANS (ASBP)
7430 E. Caley Ave., Suite 210
Englewood, CO 80111
(303) 754–5731
ASBP was founded in 1950 as the National Glandular Society. Its current executive officer is James F. Merker. Its membership is open to physicians with a special interest in the study and treatment of obesity and associated conditions, and its purpose is to encourage excellence in the practice of bariatric medicine through exchange of information, re-

search and continuing education. It publishes a newsletter and a membership directory.

ANOREXIA NERVOSA AND RELATED EATING DISORDERS (ANRED)
P.O. Box 5102
Eugene, OR 97405
(503) 344–1144

ANRED was founded in 1979. Its current president is Dr. J. Bradley Rubel. Its members are anorectics and bulimics, medical and mental health professionals, school personnel, pastors and youth workers. Its objectives are to collect and disseminate information on anorexia nervosa, bulimia, and other eating disorders; and to provide support groups, medical referrals, and counseling. It conducts workshops, seminars, conferences and training programs. It operates a treatment program in conjunction with Sacred Heart Hospital in Eugene, Oregon. It conducts educational presentations for schools, civic organizations and professional organizations. It publishes newsletters, pamphlets, brochures and resource material.

BUXOM BELLES, INTERNATIONAL (BBI)
27856 Palomino Dr.
Warren, MI 48093
(313) 754–5731

Buxom Belles was founded in 1956 and its current president is Joan Klauka. It sponsors group therapy to help in weight loss, conducts weight-loss contests, holds group discussions on diets and individual problems of reducing, and bestows awards. It publishes a monthly newsletter, *Buxom Belle Courier*.

INTERNATIONAL ASSOCIATION OF EATING DISORDERS PROFESSIONALS (IAEDP)
34213 Pacific Coast Highway, Suite E
Dana Point, CA 92629
(714) 248–1150

IAEDP is an association of professional therapists who specialize in the treatment of eating disorders. It also invites other interested individuals into its membership, particularly people recovering from eating disorders and their families and friends. IAEDP has a certification program for professionals, and its founder, Shirley Klein, travels throughout the country promoting the organization and establishing local chapters.

LEAN LINE (LL)
151 New World Way
South Plainfield, NJ 07080
(201) 757-7677
Lean Line is a weight reducing program developed by Hans Fisher at Rutgers University. Weekly classes include behavior modification techniques, body toning exercises and information on nutritionally balanced diets. It conducts special in-house classes for companies.

NATIONAL ANOREXIC AID SOCIETY (NAAS)
5796 Karl Rd.
Columbus, OH 43229
(614) 895-2009
NAAS was founded in 1977 as the Anorexic Aid Society, and its program director is Arline Iannicello. Its members are anorectics, bulimics, their families, educators, doctors and mental health professionals. It provides community education programs; organizes self-help groups; compiles listings of doctors, hospitals and clinics treating the disorders; and offers information and referral services. It publishes a newsletter.

NATIONAL ASSOCIATION OF ANOREXIA NERVOSA AND ASSOCIATED DISORDERS (ANAD)
Box 7
Highland Park, IL 60035
(312) 831-3438
ANAD was founded in 1976 and its secretary is Lizabeth Cardner. It represents anorectics, bulimics and their families. It has chapters throughout the United States, Canada, Austria and Germany, and its purpose is public education about eating disorders. It promotes research and works against discrimination. It compiles information about eating disorders, conducts a referral service and early detection programs. It has a speakers' bureau and fights the marketing of dangerous dieting aids.

NATIONAL ASSOCIATION TO AID FAT AMERICANS (NAAFA)
P.O. Box 43
Bellerose, NY 11426
(916) 443-0303
NAAFA was founded in 1969 by William J. Fabrey, who is now its chairman. It promotes acceptance of fat people and encourages members to improve the low self-esteem frequently associated with being fat. It

lobbies against discrimination in advertising, employment, fashion, medicine, insurance, the media and wherever else it is found. It maintains a library both of books and clippings, presents awards and operates a speakers bureau. It publishes a monthly newsletter, teen brochures and educational pamphlets.

OVEREATERS ANONYMOUS (OA)
P.O. Box 92870
Los Angeles, CA 90009
(213) 542–8363

OA was founded in 1960 and has 7,000 local groups. Its current executive director is Ralph McIntire. Modeled on the 12 Steps program of Alcoholics Anonymous, OA seeks to help members overcome compulsive eating. It publishes newsletters, books and pamphlets as well as an international directory of local chapters.

TOPS CLUB (TAKE OFF POUNDS SENSIBLY)
P.O. Box 07360
4575 S. Fifth St.
Milwaukee, WI 53207
(414) 482–4620

TOPS was founded in 1948 and its current president is Esther S. Manz. It has 304,000 members in 11,846 international chapters. Its weight reduction methods include group therapy, competition and achievement recognition. It sponsors a research program at the Medical College of Wisconsin. It publishes a monthly newsletter.

WEIGHT WATCHERS INTERNATIONAL
800 Community Dr.
Manhassat, NY 11030
(516) 939-0400

Founded in 1963 by Jean Nidetch, it is now a commercial corporation, which at weekly meetings teaches members how to modify behavior to achieve and maintain weight loss. It licenses a brand of food products available at supermarkets and weight loss camps and spas.

LIBRARIES AND SPECIAL COLLECTIONS

In addition to local public libraries, good sources of information include college, university and medical school libraries, which will have large collections of scientific journals having articles about eating disorder research. If there are no large university or big city libraries near you, the librarian of even a small town library can help you obtain virtually any article or book published and pertaining to eating disorders through interlibrary loan.

The following libraries and organizations can help you locate much recent and interesting literature pertaining to eating disorders, much of it free of charge:

Government Printing Office–Library Program Services
North Capital and H Street NW
Washington, DC 20401
(202) 275–2051
If you are interested in obtaining books on eating disorders for your school or for a non–profit organization, your congressman can help you obtain surplus or duplicate books from the Library of Congress, or you can contact the library directly at the address below:

Gift and Exchange Division
Library of Congress
Washington, DC 20540
(202) 287–6161
The Library of Congress also has a free information referral service, which can direct you to information about specific questions concerning eating disorders. It is called the National Referral Center and its phone number is (202) 287–5670.

National Information Clearinghouse
P.O. Box 1133
Washington, DC 20013
The Health Information Clearinghouse has specialists who can help lo-
cate information on eating disorders. They have a toll–free phone num-
ber: 800–336–4797 (in Virginia call collect (703) 522–2590).

Office of Research Reporting
National Institute of Child Health and Human Development
Building 31, Room 2A-32
National Institute of Health
9000 Rockville Pike
Bethesda, MD 20205
(301) 496-5133
A special publication, called *Obesity in Children*, can be obtained free from
this agency.

Other free information booklets can be obtained from:

Consumer Information Center
P.O. Box 100
Pueblo, CO 81002
(202) 566–1794
Some titles this center can provide include:
  About Body Wraps, Pills, and Other Magic Wands (564N). This booklet
discusses diet aids and weight loss gimmicks and their potential dangers.
  Cellulite (565N). The publication warns about gimmicks marketed sup-
posedly to help women get rid of fat on hips and thighs.
  Diet Books Sell Well But . . . (566N). This presents facts and fallacies
about fad diets and gives guidelines for selecting a healthy weight loss
diet.
  The Gender Gap at the Dinner Table (524N). Men's and women's nutritional needs differ; this publication discusses nutritional disorders and
provides weight and energy expenditure charts.

The following organizations can provide additional information or advice on locating information: **NAAFA** maintains a library of over 200
books and 60,000 clippings related to obesity. **OA** publishes pamphlets
and booklets relating to compulsive overeating. **ANAD** and **ANRED** also
provide various kinds of free information. The addresses of the above
organizations can be found in the previous organizations section.

SPECIAL PROGRAMS FOR SCHOOLS AND ORGANIZATIONS

Many eating disorder treatment centers sponsor speakers' bureaus that feature professional eating disorder counselors who will make presentations to schools and organizations, giving basic information about eating disorders, such as recognizing the symptoms, diagnosing the conditions, finding sources of help, and deciding on the course of treatment. Often the presenters are people who themselves have suffered from eating disorders and can answer questions and concerns knowledgeably.

One good way to find a speaker on eating disorders for your school or organization is to ask your librarian for the *American Hospital Association Guide to the Health Care Field*. Look under the category of substance abuse programs to find facilities offering eating disorder treatment and pick several names of facilities located near you. Some may be located in general hospitals and others may be free-standing units or located in psychiatric hospitals. Call the public relations department and ask the facility to schedule a presentation for your school or organization. There is almost always no charge for this service; however, it is still a good idea to confirm that the program will be presented at no charge before actually inviting the speaker. If you are told there will be a cost, it is probably a good idea to call other facilities nearby with your request.

One example of how speakers' bureaus work is that of New Spirit, which has several locations in the Houston area. New Spirit provides free specialized support groups for teens and addresses issues such as family life, school, self–esteem and substance abuse, including eating disorders. Speakers' bureau topics cover a wide range of concerns from depression to cocaine addiction, to suicide, in addition to eating disorders.

BIBLIOGRAPHY

OBESITY

BOOKS

Abramson, Edward E., with contributors. *Behavioral Approaches to Weight Control*. New York: Springer Publishing, 1977.

This is a collection of papers exploring the effects of behavior modification on weight reduction and eating habits. It has extensive appendixes containing weight reduction questionnaire, weekly weight graph, menu, eating diary and case histories.

Atrens, Dale. *Don't Diet*. New York: William Morrow & Company, 1988.

The author argues against mindless dieting to achieve some ill–defined ideal weight; instead he counsels good eating habits and concentrating on managing one's life to achieve the optimum satisfaction, pointing out—along with a growing number of other anti–diet advocates—that when all other systems are working, the weight one attains becomes the ideal weight.

Bailey, Covert, and Lea Bishop. *The Fit–or–Fat Woman*. Boston: Houghton Mifflin Company, 1989.

The author has tailored his earlier *Fit–or–Fat?* program for the special physiological and metabolic needs of women. He provides the basics of sensible diet and exercise.

Barnes, Broda O., and Lawrence Galton. *Hypothyroidism: The Unsuspected Illness*. New York: Thomas Y. Crowell, 1976.

This is a complete primer on thyroid function, with emphasis on the problems of an underactive thyroid. The authors include a simple test to determine hypothyroidism, and they discuss the relation of obesity to thyroid function. However, they refer to Dr. Barnes' overweight clients in demeaning language, calling them "pachyderms" and describing one obese client as resembling "two tractor tires around a barrel."

Bennett, William, and Joel Gurin. *The Dieter's Dilemma*. New York: Basic Books, 1982.

The body weight "set–point" is described as the mechanism by which the body maintains a constant weight—the weight the body maintains, plus or minus a few pounds, "when you are not thinking about it." It operates somewhat like a thermostat; when the body weight falls below the set–point, appetite increases until the set–point body weight is reached once again. The authors make a strong case that without dieting most people are the weights nature intended them to be.

Bockar, Joyce. *The Last Best Diet Book*. New York: Stein and Day, 1980.

Dr. Bockar, a psychiatrist in Stamford, Connecticut explores ways of exposing the root causes behind the individual's obsession for food. She successfully overcame obesity after 35 years and then began counseling obese patients referred by physicians. Mostly concerned with obese women, the book offers insights into particular problems and situations that can cause compulsive eating; for example, housewives are frequently tempted to overeat simply because food is so readily available all day long. She also discusses particular eating problems women face during early childhood, during the teen years and during pregnancy.

Bruch, Hilde. *The Importance of Overweight*. New York: W.W. Norton & Company, 1968.

Dr. Bruch discusses the implications of a lifetime of dieting to maintain weight control, pointing out that these "thin fat people" continue to have the same "adjustment problems as when they were fat, but they often seem to be more insecure . . ."

Chase, Chris. *The Great American Waistline: Putting It On and Taking It Off*. New York: Coward, McCann & Geoghegan, 1981.

Ostensibly a breezy look at obesity and the shift in attitudes favoring thin female bodies over the buxom Lillian Russel–type beauties of the past, the book also covers gourmet cooking and gourmet cooks, celebrities and their problems with food, little–known facts and anecdotes about food and how to diet.

Cormilot, Alberto. *Thin Forever*. Chicago: Henry Regnery Company, 1976.

This is a behavioral modification program for weight control and gives diets, physical activity programs and questionnaires for self–assessment. The author has based much of the program on Alcoholics Anonymous and Overeaters Anonymous methods. Its lack of an index limits its usefulness.

Bibliography

Danowski. T.S. *Sustained Weight Control: The Individual Approach*. Philadelphia: F.A. Davis Co., 1969.

Another book suggesting ways of modifying behavior to achieve and maintain permanent weight loss, it discusses genetic and emotional factors in obesity.

Davis, Joe, and Lucille Enix. *The Ultimate Diet: How to Lose 5 Pounds in 7 Days Without Feeling Hungry*. New York: New American Library, 1990.

Davis is a doctor and professional body builder, who contends that in order to build lean muscle mass, most fats must be eliminated from the diet. To do so, he offers the low fat, low protein, high carbohydrate diet, along with three types of diet plans for maintaining ideal weight or losing excess fat. Caution is needed when embarking on these kinds of diets. The authors offer a questionable "pig–out" principle in which they argue that occasional bingeing is harmless and may relieve the tensions created by a highly disciplined diet. For the potential compulsive eater, that is somewhat like telling a drug addict that occasional cocaine use is acceptable.

DeClements, Barthe. *Nothing's Fair in Fifth Grade*. New York: Scholastic, n.d.

A children's book aimed at adolescents, this is the story of a fat child who achieves weight loss by successfully integrating socially with her classmates. It is something of a fantasy, but it could happen.

Ellis, Audrey. *The Kid–Slimming Book*. Chicago: Henry Regnery Company, 1976.

The author is not up–to–date on recent information about heritability of obesity, not even for 1976; however she does provide sound nutritional counseling and other common sense advice, along with menus, recipes and a calorie reference chart.

Eppright, Ercel, Pearl Swanson, and Carrold Iverson, eds. *Weight*. Ames: Iowa State College Press, 1955.

The papers in this book constitute a colloquium sponsored by Iowa State College and include some notable authors such as Ancel Keys and Jean Mayer. Several papers are concerned with aging and diet, nutrition during pregnancy and childhood nutrition and weight control.

Glenn, Morton. *How To Get Thinner Once and for All*. New York: E.P. Dutton Co., 1965.

The author talks about nutrition and life–styles as well as the role of motivation in weight control; he suggests a method of "portion control" for losing weight.

————. *But I Don't Eat That Much: A Diet Specialist Answers His Patients' Questions on "Once–and–for–All" Reducing.* New York: E.P. Dutton, 1974.

Using a question–and–answer format, Dr. Glenn discusses a broad range of factors in weight control. In addition he provides a complete diet plan and his techniques for weight reduction.

Goor, Ron, Nancy Goor, and Katherine Boyd. *The Choose to Lose Diet: A Food Lover's Guide to Permanent Weight Loss.* Boston: Houghton Mifflin, 1990.

The authors emphasize cutting down on fats and eating more carbohydrates, saying that fat calories are "fattening and carbohydrate and protein calories" in reasonable quantities are not. The most useful features of the book are its advice on how to read food labels, cook with less fat and keep a food record.

Greene, Herbert, and Carolyn Jones. *Diary of a Food Addict.* New York: Grosset & Dunlap, Publishers, 1974.

Herbert Greene, famous Broadway conductor, was 100 pounds overweight. After a traffic accident hospitalized him and forced him to lose weight, he began the struggle to deal with his compulsion and overcome his food addiction. He had considerable help from actress Carolyn Jones, whom he married after coming out of the hospital and who helped him write the book.

Hauser, Gayelord. *Gayelord Hauser's New Guide to Intelligent Reducing.* New York: Farrar, Straus and Young, 1955.

Once considered somewhat of a crank by academic nutritionists and physicians, some of Hauser's 35–year–old pronouncements concerning nutrition and weight control seem remarkably prescient. For example, he advocated concentrating on nutritional and health goals rather than specific weights, also the theme of present–day anti–diet advocates.

Hirschmann, Jane, and Carol Munter. *Overcoming Overeating.* Reading, MA: Addison–Wesley Publishing Company, 1988.

Part of the growing number of psychotherapists who see harm in fad dieting, the authors point out the psychological harm done when people diet and fail to maintain weight loss. According to them the very act of giving up dieting can have positive psychological benefits and sometimes leads to weight loss. They advise their clients to get rid of bathroom scales, stock their shelves with all the foods they like, and other acts of defiance against dieting. Readers are asked to participate in a study by filling out a questionnaire in the back of the book and sending it to the authors.

Hollis, Judi. *Fat Is a Family Affair*. Center City, MN: Hazelden Educational Materials, 1985.

The author says, "If you cope with life through food you are probably suffering what has recently been labeled an eating disorder." As the title suggests, she believes that eating disorders must be treated within the context of the family. She clearly describes and defines the relatively new approach to family therapy, dealing with "codependency." The book includes questionnaires and self–tests but has no index.

Joliffe, Norman. *Reduce and Stay Reduced on the Prudent Diet*. New York: Simon and Schuster, 1964.

This is a report of a seven–year study conducted on men in New York who followed a diet called the Prudent Diet.

Jordan, Henry, Leonard Levitz, and Gordon Kimbrell. *Eating is Okay! A Radical Approach to Successful Weight Loss: The Behavioral–Control Diet Explained in Full*. New York: Rawson Associates, 1976.

1976 was a big year for diet books based on behavior modification. The authors outline a life management program, apparently assuming that if the dieter becomes fixated on managing eating habits, there will be little time left over for gaining weight.

Katahn, Martin. *The Rotation Diet*. New York: W.W. Norton, 1986.

The author is director of the weight management program at Vanderbilt University and his diet is the result both of research and clinical experience. The "rotation" aspect of the diet simply means that women alternate caloric intake from 600 to 900 to 1200 calories per day, then start again at 600. He also discusses the importance of exercise and physical activity in weight control and includes menus and recipes.

———. *The T–Factor Diet*. New York: W.W. Norton, 1989.

The author of *The Rotation Diet* now claims, based on recent metabolic research, one can lose weight without cutting calorie intake.

Kiell, Norman, ed. *The Psychology of Obesity: Dynamics and Treatment*. Springfield, IL: Charles C. Thomas Publishing, 1973.

Articles by eating disorder specialists such as Albert J. Stunkard and Jules Hirsch explore body image and self–perception of body weight, social aspects of obesity and childhood and adolescent obesity. The authors also present a broad range of treatment theories.

Kline, Milton, et al., eds. *Obesity: Etiology, Treatment and Management.* Springfield, IL: Charles C. Thomas Publishing, 1976.

This book is highly technical. Various authors discuss scientific work relating to obesity, including tissue changes during starvation, hypnosis treatment of obesity, effects of fear and food deprivation on eating habits, as well as the social factors of obesity.

LeBow, Michael D. *Adult Obesity Therapy.* Psychology Practitioner Guidebooks. Elmsford, NY: Pergamon Press, 1989.

The central theme of this book for constructing weight reduction programs is that there is no universally effective and healthy strategy for becoming thinner. The author stresses tailoring programs for each individual.

Mahoney, Michael, and Kathryn Mahoney. *Permanent Weight Control.* New York: W.W. Norton, 1976.

A non–diet weight loss guide, this was one of the earlier books to focus on behavior modification as opposed to strict adherence to diets to achieve and maintain weight loss. The program focuses on the behavior of eating: How fast do you eat? Where do you eat? What do you think about when you eat? Do you eat when you are tense? These and other questions effecting total eating behavior are explored, and the reader is encouraged to develop eating self–control strategies based on individual problems and habits rather than adhering to diets and blanket restrictions.

Mannix, Jeffrey. *The Mannix Method: A 12–Week Program for Weight Control through Behavior Training.* New York: Richard Marek Publishers, 1979.

The Mannix method teaches life control, and therefore weight control, through behavior modification. It presents a precise program in 12 sessions over 21 days that attempts to recreate behavior patterns thin people seem to be born with.

Mayer, Jean. *Overweight: Causes, Cost and Control.* Englewood Cliffs, NJ: Prentice–Hall, 1968.

A noted nutritionist presents a comprehensive look at overweight and obesity. Intended to be useful for the professional and accessible to the lay reader, Dr. Mayer explains in plain English the often complicated relationships between food and weight gain and loss. He includes a useful question–and–answer section, which explodes myths and sheds light on common questions and misconceptions about nutrition and body weight.

————. *A Diet for Living*. New York: David McKay Company, 1975.

Despite the title, this is not a "diet book," but a book about sensible eating by one of the world's foremost authorities on the subject. In a question–and–answer section, a favorite device of Dr. Mayer, he teaches some basics of nutrition and sensible eating habits. There are several useful appendixes, giving nutrient values of foods and explaining vitamins.

Mayer, Jean, and Jeanne P. Goldberg. *Dr. Jean Mayer's Diet and Nutrition Guide*. New York: Pharos Books, 1990.

Dr. Mayer gives the latest information on nutrition, including the basics: vitamins, minerals and proteins. He discusses foodborne illnesses and special diets for health problems and how to shop and read food labels. A 28–day menu plan is included.

Orbach, Susie. *Fat Is a Feminist Issue*. New York: Paddingdon Press, 1978.

Orbach believes that many women become fat and physically unattractive because it is the only way they can get men to take them seriously, saying that women protected by fat "must deny their own sexuality in order to be seen as a person." Her book has offended numerous fat feminists.

Osman, Jack. *Thin from Within*. New York: Hart Publishing Company, 1976.

This book talks about the dangers of "yo–yo dieting" and suggests numerous behavior modification tricks to maintain weight control such as the diet contract, discovering personal "pressure valves" and others. The appendix has a lengthy table of nutritive value of the edible parts of food. Lack of an index limits the book's usefulness.

Owen, Jean Z. *It's More Fun to Be Thin*. Boston: Marshall Jones Company, 1939.

It's interesting to see how attitudes have changed during the past 50 years—and also interesting to see which things have not changed. The author of this book was a great success; she got her man. And of course she did so by successfully losing weight.

Patton, Sharon Greene. *Stop Dieting—Start Living!* New York: Dodd, Mead & Company, 1983.

Ms. Patton was trapped in a cycle familiar to most obese people: going on self–imposed diets, visiting diet doctors, buying every weight loss gimmick on the market, losing weight, then relapsing and regaining it. This is the story of how she ended her obsession about weight loss.

Polivy, Janet, and C. Peter Herman. *Breaking the Diet Habit*. New York: Basic Books, 1983.

This is an anti–diet book. The authors contend that before weight loss efforts can be successful, people must accept themselves as they are and stop looking for a magic transformation through weight loss. They further hold that unrealistically stringent diets can in themselves lead to binge eating.

R., Karen. *That First Bite*. New York: Pomerica Press, 1979.

In the tradition of 12–step programs such as Overeaters Anonymous and Alcoholics Anonymous, the author is identified only by first name and last initial. She tells what it is like to binge eat uncontrollably while trying every popular weight loss remedy, then finally discovering the support of Overeaters Anonymous.

Rucker, Ellie. *The Mayor's Diet*. Austin: Hart Graphics, 1985.

A determined individual can do almost anything humanly possible, even lose 80 pounds in seven months. The author proves that highly disciplined people can maintain weight loss.

Scobey, Joan. *Short Rations: Confessions of a Cranky Calorie–Counter*. New York: Holt, Rinehart and Winston, 1980.

In contrast to the vast majority of dieting experiences, the author was successful in following a diet prescribed by a diet specialist and has maintained her weight loss. She humorously details her experience, which was not easy, and offers helpful advice for sticking to a diet.

Simmons, Richard. *Richard Simmons' Never–Say–Diet Book*. New York: Warner Books, 1980.

This is not a diet book; it is a lighthearted but serious effort to inspire weight control through better eating habits and exercise. The author, once overweight himself, hosted a successful TV show, which sought to inspire watchers (mostly women) to exercise and develop better eating habits.

Slochower, Joyce Anne. *Excessive Eating: The Role of Emotions and Environment*. New York: Human Sciences Press, 1983.

This textbook is a technical presentation of data supporting theories of emotional causes of overeating behavior and includes chapters on anxiety, uncontrollable arousal and stress in relation to overeating.

Bibliography

Stein, Laura. *The Bloomingdale's Eat Healthy Diet.* New York: St. Martin's Press, 1986.

It could be argued that because of the "Bloomingdale's" connection, this is another fad diet; however, the author has based her regimen on sound nutritional principles and stresses a program of healthy eating as opposed to restrictive dieting. She includes a question–and–answer section and cooking strategies and recipes.

Stuart, R.B., *Act Thin, Stay Thin: New Ways to Lose Weight and Keep It Off.* New York: W.W. Norton, 1978.

The author was psychological director of Weight Watchers International, Inc. and was responsible for much of the behavior modification theory advocated by the company. He teaches ways to break the appetite chain at the earliest possible link, how to recognize when the urge to eat begins to dominate one's thinking and how to avoid situations that lead to problem eating.

Stuart, R.B., and B. Davis. *Slim Chance in a Fat World: Behavioral Control of Obesity.* Champaign, IL: Research Press Company, 1972.

With extensive notes, this book discusses the behavioral approach to weight control and the importance of physical activity.

Stuart, R.B., and B. Jacobson. *Weight, Sex, and Marriage.* New York: W.W. Norton, 1987.

The authors are marriage therapists and claim that insecure husbands sometimes block attempts by their wives to lose weight. The authors attempt to assist women to move away from the role of victim toward strategies for attaining weight goals. They use many case studies and examples.

Stunkard, Albert. *The Pain of Obesity.* Palo Alto: Bull Publishing Company, 1976.

This is a professional autobiography of the well–known authority on obesity and professor of psychiatry at the University of Pennsylvania. In it he reiterates his theories from a lifetime of work on causes and effects of obesity.

Ubell, Earl. *How to Save Your Life.* New York: Harcourt Brace Jovanovich, 1973.

The author, a science reporter for television news, attempts to teach how to change bad habits to good, particularly eating and drinking habits. His total program amounts to a life–style change. The book has many useful charts; however, the lack of an index makes it difficult to use.

Whelan, Elizabeth, and Fredrick Stare. *Panic in the Pantry: Food Facts, Fads and Fallacies.* New York: Atheneum, 1975.

This book is fun to read with its numerous *New Yorker*–type cartoons about eating. The authors present many little–known facts, such as the natural chemical content of many foods and drinks. They also debunk many food myths.

Wilson, Nancy, ed. *Obesity.* Philadelphia: F.A. Davis Company, 1969.

A collection of papers by researchers and practitioners working as obesity specialists, the subjects include an overview of the development and perpetuation of obesity, teenage obesity, appetite control, as well as survey data on population patterns of disease and body weight.

Winick, Myron. *Nutrition in Health and Disease.* New York: John Wiley & Sons, 1980.

The author is a noted professor of nutrition and pediatrics at Columbia University College of Physicians and Surgeons. His book is a primer on nutrition, and is particularly thorough in discussing the disease consequences of poor nutrition, including obesity. One valuable section discusses the use of nutrition principles in prevention and treatment of disease and overweight.

Wolman, Benjamin B., ed. *Psychological Aspects of Obesity: A Handbook.* New York: Van Norstrand Reinhold Co., 1982.

This is a textbook collection of research and lecture papers by various authors in the field. Judith Rodin's article in particular lucidly presents the psychological dilemmas of obesity management.

Wyden, Peter. *The Overweight Society.* New York: William Morrow Company, 1965.

This is not a diet book, but a commentary on social attitudes toward obesity. The author discusses fad diets of the 1960s and advocates behavioral changes to achieve weight control.

Yudkin, John. *This Nutrition Business.* New York: St. Martin's Press, 1976.

The author is an English nutritionist, and he writes clearly and sensibly about food, eating habits, additives and agricultural practices affecting sound nutrition, overeating and diet and disease.

PERIODICALS

Beck, Melinda, and others. "The Losing Formula." *Newsweek* April 30, 1990:52.

This article, on the liquid diet craze, includes some up–to–date and disturbing statistics, including the following: in 1990 20 million Americans will spend $1 billion on medically supervised liquid diet products; as many as half the people who sign up for these diets don't complete them; and people who lose weight rapidly are three times more likely to regain it than those who diet slowly. The article is a good overview of current trends in the weight loss industry.

Bell, C. S. Kirkpatrick, and R. Rinn. 1986, "Body Image of Anorexic, Obese, and Normal Females." *Journal of Clinical Psychology* 42:431–439 (1986).

The overweight underestimate the degree of obesity in their body self–image.

Blumenthal, Deborah. 1988. "Dieting Reassessed." *The New York Times Magazine* Oct. 8, 1988:S24.

Brownell, Kelly, 1988. "Yo–Yo Dieting: Repeated Efforts to Lose Weight Can Give You a Hefty Problem." *Psychology Today* January 1988:20.

Bruch, Hilde. 1961. "Conceptual Confusion in Eating Disorders." *Journal of Nervous and Mental Disease* 133:46–54.

In one of the author's earlier works, she begins to interpret children's struggle with weight control as part of developmental difficulties with autonomy and the sense of self.

Canning, Helen, and Jean Mayer. 1966. "Obesity—Its Possible Effect on College Acceptance." *New England Journal of Medicine* 275:1172–74.

Overweight applicants were found to have a lower rate of admission to college, obese girls' acceptance rates being lower than obese boys'.

Castelnovo–Tedesco, P., and L. Reiser. 1988. "Compulsive Eating: Obesity and Related Phenomena." *Journal of the American Psychoanalytic Association* 36:163–171.

This paper describes personality traits frequently found in obese people; they may use food as a panacea for disappointment.

Chirico, Anna–Marie, and Albert Stunkard. 1960. "Physical Activity and Human Obesity." *New England Journal of Medicine* 263:935–40.

The authors compared activity levels of both obese and nonobese subjects. Using pedometers. they discovered that lean women walked more than twice as much as fat women. Obese and nonobese males showed a much smaller variation.

Council on Scientific Affairs. 1988. "Treatment of Obesity in Adults." *JAMA, The Journal of the American Medical Association* 260:2547.

This is a survey report on treatment methods.

Cox, James, and Terry L. Powley. 1977. "Development of Obesity in Diabetic Mice Pair–Fed with Lean Siblings." *Journal of Comparative and Physiological Psychology* 91:347–58.

This study confirmed some aspects of the genetic role in the development of obesity.

Dane, Abe. 1989. "Flab–to–Muscle Pill? Experimental Drug Revs Up Fat Metabolism." *American Health: Fitness of the Body and Mind* July–August, 1989:18.

DeFrank, Thomas N. 1989. "Tales from the Diet Trenches." *Newsweek* September 11, 1989:58.

Donovan, Jennifer Boeth, and June Bailey. 1987. "I Weigh 220 Pounds and I'm Glad." *Woman's Day* March 24, 1987:42.

Not all obese women want to lose weight.

Einstein, Laurie. 1988. "Exercising Your Calories Away!" *Current Health* December 1988:25.

This is an exercise regimen designed to keep you slim.

Fackelmann, Kathy A. 1989. "Weight Loss Builds a Healthy Liver." *Science News* May 2, 1989:332.

Foreyt, J. 1987. "Issues in the Assessment and Treatment of Obesity." *Journal of Consulting and Clinical Psychology* 55:677–684.

The author describes health risks of obesity: cardiovascular disease, hypertension and diabetes.

Gage, Diane, and Noonie Benford. 1988. "Robot Dieting." *American Health* May 1988:138.

Yet another dieting device is tried, this time a mouth guard designed to make eating difficult.

Golin, Mark. 1989. "Psych Yourself Slim: 10 Dos and Don'ts for Pounds–Off Success." *Prevention* May 1989:108.

Gordon, Linda. 1988. "The Secret is Keeping Off the Weight You Lost." *Glamour* June 1988:132.

The women's magazines are beginning to recognize that dieting is not enough. It's maintaining weight loss that counts.

Bibliography

Gurin, Joel. 1989. "Leaner, Not Lighter: Why You Need to Rethink Your Beliefs About Dieting Before You Start." *Psychology Today* June 1989:32.

Herman, C. Peter, and Deborah Mack. 1975. "Restrained and Unrestrained Eating." *Journal of Personality* 43:647–60.

This is an important study that first correlated the eating behaviors of restrained vs. unrestrained eaters (i.e., dieters vs. nondieters) as opposed to fat vs. thin subjects.

Horosko, Marian. 1988. "Optical Delusion: Optical Delusion: Optical Delusion: Mirror, Mirror, on the Studio Wall, Who's the Thinnest One of All?" *Dance Magazine* June 1988:60.

Howard, Elizabeth Meade. 1988. "Lynn Redgrave's Diet Tips: The Lovely Star a Former Fattie!" *McCall's* February 1988:88.

The article tells how Ms. Redgrave is now able to remain slim.

Kinter, M., P. Boss, and N. Johnson. 1981. "The Relationship between Dysfunctional Family Environments and Family Member Food Intake." *Journal of Marriage and The Family* 43:633–641.

Kolotkin, R., E. Revis, B. Kirkley, and L. Janick. 1987. "Binge Eating in Obesity: Associated MMPI Characteristics." *Journal of Consulting and Clinical Psychology* 55:872–876.

Binge eaters may perceive themselves as having little self control. It is estimated that one–third to one–half of the obese seeking treatment are binge eaters.

Koontz, Katy. 1988. "Women Who Love Food Too Much." *Health* February 1988:40.

Levine, Beth, and Jean Crichton. 1988. "Diet and Fitness Books." *Publishers Weekly* March 25, 1988:168.

This is a bibliography, a quick and easy way to screen lots of books on diet and fitness.

Lieberman, Alex. 1989. "Turning a 'Dark Day' into Triumph." *Prevention* December 1989:100.

Inspirational story of a woman diet pill "junkie" who turned life around and lost weight after she learned pills had damaged her gallbladder.

Lieberman, Alexis. 1988. "She's Doing a Victory Dance." *Prevention* December 1988:80.

This is the story of a body make over, including weight loss.

Lindner, Lawrence. 1989. "Type A Diet Traps: Keeping Your Life in Perfect Order May Work Against Weight-Loss Success." *Health* August 1989:36.

Maddox, George, and Veronica Liederman. 1969. "Overweight as a Social Disability with Medical Implications." *Journal of Medical Education* 44:214–20.

The authors found that doctors as well as laymen expressed negative biases against the obese.

Marcus, M., R. Wing, and J. Hopkins. 1988. "Obese Binge Eaters: Affect, Cognitions, and Response to Behavioral Weight Control." *Journal of Consulting and Clinical Psychology* 56:433–439.

One–third to one–half of the obese who seek treatment are binge eaters.

Mayer, Jean, Purnima Roy, and Kamakhya Prasad Mitra. 1956. "Relation Between Caloric Intake, Body Weight, and Physical Work." *American Journal of Clinical Nutrition* 4:169–75.

Dr. Mayer and his colleagues established the relationship of physical activity to the maintenance of body weight.

Neale, Susan. 1987. "The Advice Diet Counselors Fork Out." *Changing Times* June 1987:67.

Neill, John, John Marshall, and Charles Yale. 1978. "Marital Changes after Intestinal Bypass Surgery." *Journal of the American Medical Association* 240:447–50.

The authors' study found that after weight loss resulting from surgery, spouses of slimmed–down subjects felt increased insecurity because of their partners new sexual attractiveness.

Pearce, J., M. LeBow, and J. Orchard. 1981. "Role of Spouse Involvement in the Behavioral Treatment of Overweight Women." *Journal of Consulting and Clinical Psychology* 49:236–244.

Piercy, Marge. 1988. "My, Haven't You Lost Weight!" *Woman's Day* October 25, 1989:225.

In this column, the author talks about society's undue emphasis on looks.

Prevention, editors of. 1989. "She Reaches for Her Pen." *Prevention* October 1989:107.

A woman who had been on the diet merry–go–round for 30 years learns how to maintain weight loss by keeping a journal.

Bibliography

Rand, Colleen. 1979. "Obesity and Human Sexuality." *Medical Aspects of Human Sexuality* 13 (January 1979):140–52.

The author reviewed psychiatric evaluations of obese subjects awaiting surgery for weight control and others and found that "There are no data which indicate that the obese individual has significantly greater or fewer sexual problems than nonobese individuals."

Richardson, S.A., N. Goodman, A.H. Hastorf, and S.M. Dornbusch. 1961. "Cultural Uniformity in Reaction to Physical Disabilities." *American Sociological Review* 26:241–47.

This study asked respondents to rate degrees of attractiveness to various deformities in children including missing limbs and facial disfigurations as well as obesity. Fat children were rated the least attractive.

Roberts, Andrea. 1987. "We Lost 239 Lbs." *Seventeen* May 1987:166.

This story is about several girls who have successfully lost weight.

Rodale, Heidi. 1988. "She Took the Pressure Off Her Health." *Prevention* March 1988:55.

A related article in the same issue talks about weight loss and blood pressure.

Seligmann, Jean. 1987. "The Littlest Dieters: Many Normal–Size Kids Are Counting Calories." *Newsweek* July 27, 1987:48.

Related articles in the same issue tell about instilling good eating habits in children.

————. 1988. "Helping Fight Extra Helpings: Food Junkies Are Turning to OA to Kick Their Habit." *Newsweek* December 5, 1988:78.

This is a feature story about OA and how it works.

Schachter, Stanley, Ronald Goldman, and Andrew Gordon. 1968. "Effects of Fear, Food Deprivation, and Obesity on Eating." *Journal of Personality and Social Psychology* 10:91–97.

The study found, among other things, that fat people did not overeat as a response to fear or anxiety.

Schwartz, Hillel. 1987. "Being Thin Isn't Always Being Happy." *U.S. News & World Reports* February 9, 1987:74.

The author interviews people on the reasons they diet.

Schwartzberg, Neala S. 1990. "Do I Look Fat?" *Parent's Magazine* January 1990:66.

Simon, Robin, and Bob Grohne. 1988. "Walking for Weight Loss—and a Whole Lot More." *Prevention* September 13, 1988:54.

Stevens, Carole. 1988. "It's Not Your Fault: Your Body's Slow Metabolism Could Be the Reason It's So Hard to Lose Weight." *Washingtonian* October 1989:83.

Stuart, Richard. 1967. "Behavioral Control of Overeating." *Behavior Research and Therapy* 5:357–65.

This article reports on the research that established behavior modification as an important element of the management of weight control.

Stunkard, Albert. 1959. "Obesity and the Denial of Hunger." *Psychosomatic Medicine* 4:281–89.

In this study the author found that while nonobese women readily admitted to hunger, obese women regularly denied hunger even when stomach contractions indicated they clearly were.

Trillin, Calvin. 1971. "U.S. Journal." *The New Yorker* 47 (July 3, 1971):57–63.

The subject is Larry "Fats" Goldberg, a New York pizza restaurant owner who successfully reduced by 160 pounds and kept the weight off; however, he tells of experiencing perpetual hunger.

Waxman, Marjorie, and Albert Stunkard. 1980. "Caloric Intake and Expenditure of Obese Boys." *Journal of Pediatrics* 2:187–93.

This study found that obese children were inactive at home, but at school got a normal amount of exercise and because of their weight burned a greater number of calories than their leaner schoolmates.

Webb, Denise. 1990. "When the Pounds Stop Coming Off: How the Experts Cope with the Dieting Plateaus." *The New York Times* February 21, 1990:B5, C4.

Weinberg, Norris, Myer Mendelson, and Albert Stunkard. 1957. "A Failure to Find Distinctive Personality Features in a Group of Obese Men." *American Journal of Psychiatry* 117:1035–37.

Attempting to confirm the generally held belief that the obese were more neurotic than the nonobese, the authors failed to find any evidence to support the belief.

FILMS

For Tomorrow We Shall Diet. 16 mm, 24 min. 1976. Churchill Films.

A young woman attempts to change her eating habits. The film tells of the danger of fad dieting and gives information on the importance of good nutrition and exercise.

Bibliography

ANOREXIA
BOOKS

Bell, Rudolph M. 1986. *Holy Anorexia.* Chicago: University of Chicago Press.

The phenomenon of severely fasting religious zealots was fairly common in medieval Italy, somewhat in the way anorexia nervosa is common in the United States today. Catherine of Siena literally starved herself to death at the age of 33, in spite of countermeasures by her family. The author concludes that much of this phenomenon was the result of young women's need for autonomy, and self–starvation represented the needed control.

Bruch, Hilde. 1978. *The Golden Cage: The Enigma of Anorexia Nervosa.* Cambridge, MA: Harvard University Press.

This is the book all other eating disorders professionals refer to as being the definitive description of anorexia nervosa, its symptoms, its treatment and the psychological factors leading to its onset. Bruch uses case histories to illustrate her theories. Before her death in 1984, Hilde Bruch was widely regarded as the foremost expert in understanding and treating eating disorders.

———. 1988. *Conversations with Anorexics.* Edited by Danita Czyzewski and Melanie A. Suhr. New York: Basic Books.

Dr. Bruch's course of treatment, which focused on family dynamics, is presented by the editors. Dr. Bruch's conversations with her patients are in down–to–earth language that allows the reader to experience the same insights available to the patients themselves as they began to understand their problems with eating.

Brumberg, Joan Jacobs. 1988. *Fasting Girls: The Emergence of Anorexia Nervosa as a Modern Disease.* Cambridge, MA: Harvard University Press.

This is a social and cultural history of the disorder. The author traces its causes to the rise of the middle class, beginning with the Victorian era, and calls it a disorder of "food abundance." Robust women in Victorian times were thought to look "working class," and middle–class women would starve themselves to become thin so as to not be mistaken for working–class. The author also explores anorexia mirabilis (miraculously inspired loss of appetite), a medieval expression of piety practiced by St. Catherine of Siena, pillar saints and others.

Chernin, Kim. 1981. *The Obsession: Reflections on the Tyranny of Slenderness.* New York: Harper & Row.

The subtitle describes the book very well. Ms. Chernin claims that weight obsession is related to the "hidden emotional life of a woman." She explores the reasons for the social obsession leading to a near epidemic of anorexia nervosa among women in our age. She also suggests that the reasons for the rise of father–daughter incest and child pornography may be rooted in male hostility toward the women's movement.

Crisp. A.H. 1980. *Anorexia Nervosa: Let Me Be.* New York: Grune & Stratton.

This book, relatively short considering its thoroughness, presents a view of anorexia nervosa from the perspective of a specialist working in England. The book covers the background of the disorder's emergence from early childhood eating and social experiences, maturational crises, through behavioral and physical features of the condition. He presents a section on intervention and self–help including diagnosis, self–help techniques, factors affecting outcome and the perspective of the patients themselves. There is a useful appendix, giving average body weights at different ages and heights. This book is frequently cited in bibliographies of other authors.

Garfield, Paul E., and David M. Garner. 1982. *Anorexia Nervosa: A Multidimensional Perspective.* New York: Brunner/Mazel, Publishers.

The authors present a clinical picture of anorexia nervosa, beginning with diagnosis and explaining various subtypes of the disorder. They discuss physiological aspects of body weight, such as the pituitary gland and the function of the hypothalamus; sociocultural factors leading to anorexia; and the role of the family. They discuss management of the disease including hospitalization and psychotherapy.

Landau, Elaine. 1983. *Why Are They Starving Themselves: Understanding Anorexia Nervosa and Bulimia.* New York: Julian Messner.

Written especially for teenagers, this book presents vivid case histories of anorexia nervosa and bulimia that all teenagers can relate to. The book is especially aimed to help teenagers understand the factors leading to these eating disorders.

Levenkron, Steven. 1982. *Treating and Overcoming Anorexia Nervosa.* New York: Warner Books.

This prominent therapist specializes in the treatment and study of anorexia nervosa. Using case histories, he presents a more aggressive treatment, which he calls nurturant–authoritative psychotherapy, than the traditional passive therapy. His novel, *The Best Little Girl in the World*, was made into a TV movie.

Bibliography

Orbach, Susie. 1986. *Hunger Strike: The Anorectic's Struggle as a Metaphor for Our Age.* New York: W.W. Norton.

The author, a feminist, relates anorexia nervosa to current social trends and thus develops her "metaphor" as society's preoccupation with food, fashion and thinness. She also covers medical aspects and treatment.

PERIODICALS

Aponte, H., and J. Hoffman. 1973. "The Open Door: A Structural Approach to a Family with an Anorectic Child." *Family Process* 12:1–44.

This article discusses a videotape of an initial interview with a family of an anorectic in which a connection is made between the child's anorexia and the family's structural organization.

Appelo, Tim. 1988. "Young Women Wasting Away." *Savvy* May 1988:18.

Barcai, A. 1971. "Family Therapy and Treatment of Anorexia Nervosa." *American Journal of Psychiatry* 128:286–290.

Family therapy enables a family to change patterns preventing an anorectic member from gaining weight. The resulting weight gain allows therapy to focus on family conflicts and process rather than on the weight gain itself.

Caille, P., P. Abrahamsen, and C. Girolami. 1977. "A Systems Theory Approach to a Case of Anorexia Nervosa." *Family Process* 16:455–465.

Sometimes dysfunctional families use a behavior or mental deviation of one member as a crutch in preventing family disintegration.

Conrad, D.E. 1977. "A Starving Family: An Interactional View of Anorexia Nervosa." *Bulletin of the Menninger Clinic* 41:487–495.

This is a case history of an anorectic patient in which treatment is described.

Crisp, A.H. 1988. "Some Possible Approaches to Prevention of Eating Disorders with Particular Reference to Anorexia Nervosa." *The International Journal of Eating Disorders* January 1988:1.

Greenberg, Joel. 1985. "Researchers Identify 'Cancer Anorexia.' " *Science News* August 31, 1985:132.

Some cancer patients develop a specific type of anorexia that appears to be a learned aversion to specific foods associated with their illness or with chemotherapy treatments.

Kolata, Gina. 1986. "Depression, Anorexia, Cushing's Link Revealed." *Science* June 6, 1986:1197.

Persons with depression, anorexia nervosa and Cushing's disease all produce excess cortisol, a stress hormone. They also share some symptoms such as sleep disorders and loss of appetite.

Oyebode, F., J.A. Boodhoo, and K. Schapira. 1988. "Anorexia Nervosa in Males: Clinical Features and Outcome." *The International Journal of Eating Disorders* January 1988:121.

Anorexia nervosa in males has not been well studied. The authors are beginning to correct the oversight.

Rogak, Lisa. 1986. "Why Does He Want to Starve?" *Weight Watchers* June, 1986:61.

This is one of the few articles appearing in a popular magazine that takes a look at the problem of anorexia nervosa in men.

Rosman, B.L., S. Minuchin, and R. Liebman. 1975. "Family Lunch Sessions: An Introduction to Family Therapy in Anorexia Nervosa." *American Journal of Orthopsychiatry* 45:846–853.

The authors advocate using family lunch time in diagnosing and treating anorexia nervosa and cite data demonstrating success of method.

Wold, P. 1973. "Family Structure in Three Cases of Anorexia Nervosa: The Role of the Father." *American Journal of Psychiatry* 130:1394–1397.

In these cases the anorectic's weight loss is an expression of hostility toward the father.

FILMS AND TAPES

Diet unto Death: Anorexia Nervosa. 13 min. 1980. MTI Teleprograms.

Four young women speak frankly about their efforts to overcome anorexia nervosa. The film tells how to get help for treatment and lists treatment facilities and organizations.

Dieting—The Danger Point. With teacher's guide. 1979. Del Mar, CA: CRM–McGraw Hill Films.

This film examines the physical and psychological dangers of overdieting. It shows the near epidemic number of bright and otherwise healthy teens who are caught up in the current craze to be thin.

Minuchin, S. *Interview with a Teenage Anorectic Patient and Her Family*. New York: South Beach Psychiatric Center.

This tape shows the author taking a case history from the family, demonstrating history–taking techniques. It reveals the anorexia as a symptom of a power struggle within the family.

Bibliography

BULIMIA
BOOKS

Arenson, Gloria. 1984. *Binge Eating: How to Stop It Forever*. New York: Rawson Associates.

This is a four–step program designed to bring binge eating under control. The book is based on a successful workshop program the author has used at the Eating Disorders Treatment Center in Los Angeles and elsewhere that aims to help regain control of eating behavior. She uses many case histories to demonstrate her philosophy, and she recommends keeping a food diary, which will reveal events that trigger compulsive eating. The author was once a binge eater, and in an important and useful section, tells what aid close friends and family can give to the binge eater. The book has an excellent reading list that covers more than just eating disorder books.

Boskind–White, Marlene, and William White. 1987. *Bulimarexia: The Binge/Purge Cycle*. New York: W.W. Norton & Company.

This is an updated edition of a 1983 book with additional findings about the physiological consequences of binge eating and the relationship of dieting to eating disorders. The authors discuss treatment—individual and group therapy, as well as treatment of families and couples. Important new work in on–campus prevention programs is also discussed.

Hall, Lindsey, and Leigh Cohn. 1986. *Bulimia: A Guide to Recovery*. Santa Barbara: Gurze Books.

A short paperback, this book gives practical suggestions about how to get help. It also provides a guide for conducting support groups.

Hawkins, Raymond C., et al., eds. 1984. *The Binge–Purge Syndrome*. New York: Springer Publishing Company.

Various authors discuss the diagnosis of bulimia and its relation to anorexia nervosa; recent research and current theory about bulimia; and its assessment and treatment.

Pope, Harrison G. Jr., and James I. Hudson. 1984. *New Hope for Binge Eaters: Advances in the Understanding and Treatment of Bulimia*. New York: Harper & Row.

Using case histories, the author explains the onset and progression of the disorders and recommends approaches to seeking help. He includes simple self–tests and a question–and–answer section. He relates bulimia to other psychological disorders. Notes are extensive.

Root, Maria P.P., Patricia Fallon, and William N. Friedrich. 1986. *Bulimia: A Systems Approach to Treatment*. New York: W.W. Norton.

This book defines bulimia, explores its sociocultural causes, family systems in which it is found—such as the perfect family, the overprotective family and the chaotic family—and discusses various treatment methods such as individual therapy, couples therapy and group therapy as well as treatment of bulimic families.

Rowland, Cynthia. 1984. *The Monster Within: Overcoming Bulimia*. Grand Rapids, MI: Baker Book House.

Television news reporter Cynthia Rowland suffered secretly from bulimia, successfully hiding her disorder from friends and co–workers. Only after becoming suicidal and near death from electrolyte imbalance did she seek help at an eating disorders clinic. This book is her diary of that experience.

PERIODICALS

"Busting the Bulimia 'Epidemic.' " *Science News* (July 27, 1985) 128:56.

The bulimia epidemic among university women is much less than once thought, but incidence of bulimia is greater among university women than working women.

Bwer, Bruce. 1987. "How Effective are Bulimia Treatments?" *Science News* October 31, 1987:278.

Cerrato, Paul. 1987. "Helping Food Addicts Kick the Habit." *RN* 50:75.

Directed to nurses, this column tells how to recognize signs of bulimia and how to intervene to help patients overcome their behavior.

Cooper, J.L., T.L. Morrison, O.L. Bigman, S.I. Abramowitz, D. Blunden, A. Nassi, and P. Krener. 1988. "Bulimia and Borderline Personality Disorder." *The International Journal of Eating Disorders* January 1988:43.

Borderline personality disorder has been found in large numbers of bulimics seeking treatment.

Gray, J. J., K. Kord, and L. M. Kelly. 1987. "The Prevalence of Bulimia in a Black College Population." *The Journal of International Eating Disorders* November 1987:733.

Some ethnic groups, such as blacks, are especially prone to become overweight, and thus also prone to develop bulimia.

Herzog, David, and Paul M. Copeland. 1988. "Bulimia Nervosa—Psyche and Satiety." *New England Journal of Medicine* 319:716.

This is an editorial on the psychological and biological factors of bulimia, citing the numbers of young women who become bulimic during efforts to lose weight.

Life, editors of. 1987. "The Body Prison; A Bulimic's Compulsion to Eat More, Eat Less, Add Muscle, Get Thinner." *Life* February 1987:44.

In an issue devoted to fitness, this is the personal story of a young bulimic girl and her experience at the Renfrew Center in Philadelphia, the first residential treatment facility for eating disorders.

Mitchell, P. B. 1988. "The Pharmacological Management of Bulimia Nervosa: A Critical Review." *The International Journal of Eating Disorders* January 1988:29.

This is a review of the various drugs given in an effort to lessen bulimic behavior.

O'Donnell, Michael. 1986. "A Food Malady that Likes Upwardly Mobile Women." *International Management* October 1986:104.

Schotte, David, and Albert Stunkard. 1987. "Bulimia vs. Bulimic Behaviors on a College Campus." *JAMA, The Journal of the American Medical Association* 258:1213.

This study helps explode the myth that bulimia is epidemic on college campuses. In a self–report survey of 1965 students at an Eastern university only 1.3% of women and 0.1% of men were found to be bulimic.

Wilson, G. Terence, and L. Lindholm. 1987. "Bulimia Nervosa and Depression." *The International Journal of Eating Disorders* November 1987:725.

As the title suggests, the authors have examined the role of depression in the development of bulimia.

EATING DISORDERS, GENERAL
BOOKS

Abrahamson, E.M., and A.W. Pezet. 1951. *Body, Mind, and Sugar*. New York: Holt, Rinehart and Winston.

Though an old book, this is a well–told story of hyperinsulinism and its relation and resemblance to diabetes. Hyperinsulinism was later linked to obesity caused by adult onset diabetes.

B., Bill. 1981. *Compulsive Overeater: The Basic Text for Compulsive Overeaters.* Minneapolis: CompCare Publications.

Patterned closely on the Alcoholics Anonymous publication, *Twelve Steps and Twelve Traditions,* this book attempts to do for Overeaters Anonymous what the 12–steps book did for AA, which was to become the basic textbook to be used and cited by all members and to provide a written reference guide for the program nationally.

Beatties, Melody. 1989. *Beyond Codependency: and Getting Better All the Time.* New York: Harper & Row.

Beattie deals with the usual co–dependency topics of oneself and one's needs, family of origin, intimacy, boundaries, conflict resolution, children and relationships. She calls co–dependency a term applying to any "person who has let someone else's behavior affect him or her, and is obsessed with controlling that person's behavior."

Berger, Stuart. 1987. *How to Be Your Own Nutritionist.* New York: William Morrow and Company, Inc.

Just as the title suggests, the author advocates that each person should learn enough about nutrition to "write your own prescription for vital health and energy." In addition to being a primer on nutrition, the book has a reference section about vitamins and minerals.

Berland, Theodore. and the Editors of Consumer Guide. N.d. *Rating the Diets: Everything You Should Know about the Diets Making News.* Skokie, IL: Consumer Guide.

This book is a good place to find out about lots of popular diets in one place. In addition, the editors rate and recommend them according to several criteria such as safety and nutritional balance.

Berne, Eric. 1964. *Games People Play: The Psychology of Human Relationships.* New York: Grove Press.

The "games" people play are frequently part of the patterns of manipulation inherent in many personal relationships. Although not known at the time Dr. Berne wrote the book, co–dependent relationships are rife with these manipulative games.

Bradshaw, John. 1988. *Bradshaw On: The Family. A Revolutionary Way of Self–Discovery.* Deerfield Beach, FL: Health Communications, Inc.

This book is based on the author's television series "Bradshaw On: The Family" and "Eight Stages of Man." He claims that 96% of all families are to some degree emotionally impaired, and the dysfunctions are handed down from generation to generation and to society as a whole. His purpose here is to heal families, thus breaking the inter-generational patterns.

————. 1988. *Healing the Shame That Binds You*. Deerfield Beach, FL: Health Communications.

The author claims that shame is at the core of problems of compulsions, co–dependency and addictions. Working through affirmations, visualizations, one's "inner voice" and feelings, he helps to guide his clients out of their shame and into a healing process.

Brody, Jane. 1982. *Jane Brody's Nutrition Book*. New York: Bantam Books.

This is a commonsense approach to eating and food selection and preparation, giving the nutritional consequences of various dietary selections. Written in simple nontechnical language, it is nonetheless comprehensive.

Brownell, Kelly, and John Foreyt, eds. 1986. *Handbook of Eating Disorders: Physiology, Psychology, and Treatment of Obesity, Anorexia, and Bulimia*. New York: Basic Books.

This important book is a comprehensive reference to the three major eating disorders, and its contributors are the foremost authorities in the field. Articles cover all aspects of the disorders, from diagnosis to treatment. Clinical examples are useful to both researchers and clinicians.

Bruch, Hilde. 1973. *Eating Disorders; Obesity, Anorexia Nervosa, and the Person Within*. New York: Basic Books.

This book was one of the first by a nationally respected practitioner and teacher to examine the psychological underpinnings of eating disorders in such a way to begin the development of successful treatment regimens.

Caplan, Paula J. 1989. *Don't Blame Mother: Mending the Mother–Daughter Relationship*. New York: Harper & Row.

This is a self–help book that explores the mother–daughter relationship—almost always a relevant factor in the development of eating disorders. She stresses the importance of daughters understanding biases, the tradition of motherhood and other forces that shaped their mothers' lives. It has an extensive bibliography.

Cermak, Timmen L. 1986. *Diagnosing and Treating Co–Dependence: A Guide for Professionals Who Work with Chemical Dependents, Their Spouses and Children*. Minneapolis: Johnson Institute Books.

The author's concept of co–dependence assumes that addiction is a family disease "in the most profound sense of the word. Sooner or later, everyone around the sick person 'catches' it in one form or another." Although this book is aimed at professionals, the author's non-technical style and his use of myths and other stories for illustration make the book accessible to nonprofessionals.

Cheraskin, Emanuel, and W.M. Ringsdorf Jr. (with Arlene Brecher). 1976. *Psychodietetics: Food as the Key to Emotional Health*. New York: Bantam Books.

Research that connects diet with emotional states and attempts to promote mental health through diet is described. The authors claim that food can cause emotional illness and that dieting can drive one crazy.

Clark, Jean Illsley, and Connie Dawson. 1989. *Growing Up Again: Parenting Ourselves, Parenting Our Children*. New York: Harper & Row.

Parents who themselves were raised in dysfunctional homes often become part of the vicious cycle if they do not learn parenting skills that can give their children what was lacking in their own childhoods. The book uses charts, illustrations and exercises to help parents learn skills such as implementing discipline and structure, setting limits and showing love.

Connors, C. Keith. 1989. *Feeding the Brain: How Foods Affect Children*. New York: Plenum Publishing.

If eating disorders are to be understood fully, the interactions between certain foods and infants will need to be understood fully. This book reviews and interprets scientific studies on sugar, hyperactivity and aggression, breakfast composition and artificial sweetners. It also critiques fads such as megavitamin therapy.

Cooper, Robert K. 1989. *Health and Fitness Excellence: The Scientific Action Plan*. Boston: Houghton Mifflin Company.

This is a general health book although it does stress body fat control as well as basic nutrition, presented in seven steps.

Damon, Albert, ed. 1975. *Physiological Anthropology*. New York: Oxford University Press.

The chapter by Marshall T. Newman on nutritional adaptation in man examines the evolution of the biological and cultural aspects of human eating behavior. From the anthropologist's point of view it also discusses world food supply and effects of both undernutrition in poor countries and overnutrition in highly developed countries.

Bibliography

Diamond, Harvey and Marilyn. 1985. *Fit for Life*. New York: Warner Books.

The authors advocate a holistic approach to eating instead of dieting. Their program describes three principles essential to allow the body to control and maintain its own desirable weight level: the principle of high water content food, the principle of proper food combining and the principle of correct fruit consumption. Although unorthodox, the book has the endorsement of several prominent doctors.

Dowling, Colette. 1981. *The Cinderella Complex: Women's Hidden Fear of Independence*. New York: Pocket Books.

As the title and subtitle suggest, the author contends that the pre–liberated woman allowed herself to be oppressed, much like Cinderella. The result has been many inner conflicts, causing a variety of emotional problems.

Dufty, William. 1975. *Sugar Blues*. New York: Warner Books.

It was Dufty, protégé of actress Gloria Swanson, who first suggested to the general public that sugar was addictive. He wrote this book 15 years after having kicked the sugar habit, and he shares the results of his research on sugar. He also gives recipes for sugar–free foods.

Dyer, Wayne, 1978. *Pulling Your Own Strings*. New York: Thomas Y. Crowell Company.

Many people choose the victim role for themselves. The author shows how to avoid victimization and how to break habits that lead to victimization. Some of his chapter titles include: "Declaring Yourself as a Non–Victim"; "Refusing to Be Seduced by What is Over or Cannot Be Changed"; and "Teaching Others How You Want to Be Treated."

Ebbitt, Joan. 1987. *The Eating Illness Workbook*. Park Ridge, IL: Parkside Medical Services Corporation.

Many of the problems of disordered eating are the patterns of behavior relating to how, when, what and why one eats. Workbook exercises focus on subjects such as body image, accepting one's body and the problem of obsession.

Eden, Alvin, with Joan Heilman. 1980. *Dr. Eden's Diet and Nutrition Program for Children*. New York: Hawthorn/Dutton.

Dr. Eden's program is designed to help parents control children's weights and establish "thin" eating habits. It has menus divided into age groups and two handy appendixes giving calorie counts of common foods. An earlier version of this book was called *Growing Up Thin*, published in 1975.

Edwards, Sandra. 1981. *Too Much Is Not Enough: An Insider's Answer to Compulsive Eating*. New York: McGraw–Hill Book Company.

Both the personal testimony of the author's own compulsive eating and a wider examination of the literature relating to the disorder helps this book clarify an important aspect of eating disorders: uncontrollable overeating or bingeing.

Ellis, Albert, with Janet L. Wolfe and Sandra Mosely. 1966. *How to Prevent Your Child from Becoming a Neurotic Adult*. New York: Crown.

The famous psychologist discusses all aspects of childhood psychology, including eating behavior. He advises parents how to handle most typical childhood behavioral problems in order to produce a neurosis–free adult. His advice about eating problems is largely commonsense suggestions most parents are already familiar with.

Emmett, Steven Wiley. 1985. *Theory and Treatment of Anorexia Nervosa and Bulimia: Biomedical, Sociocultural, and Psychological Perspective*. New York: Brunner/Mazel Publishers.

This is a collection of papers from researchers and practitioners giving biomedical, sociocultural and historical perspectives, as well as innovative treatment techniques and theoretical models including group therapy within families of bulimics, a reparenting model and inpatient treatment programs. It presents results of recent studies as well.

Faulkner, Paul. 1986. *Making Things Right When Things Go Wrong: Ten Proven Ways to Put Your Life in Order*. Ft. Worth: Sweet Publishing.

More self–help to allow individuals, such as the overeater and others whose lives are out of control, to bring discipline and order to daily living. Dr. Faulkner's strategies aim to help the reader stay on track in working toward dreams, making anger work productively and mending broken relationships.

Fishel, Ruth. 1988. *Learning to Live in the Now: 6–Week Personal Plan to Recovery*. Pompano Beach, FL: Health Communications, Inc.

Using meditation, affirmations, visualizations and other exercises, the author leads the reader through a personal 6–week plan to foster self–knowledge and bring a heightened awareness to the here and now.

Fonda, Jane, with Mignon McCarthy. 1984. *Women Coming of Age*. New York: Simon & Schuster.

Bibliography

Basically a woman's reference guide to growing older, this book covers all aspects of caring for the body, emphasizing exercise for controlling weight as well as sound nutrition. There is a useful Resource Guide, listing books, organizations and programs aimed at helping women.

Forward, Susan, with Craig Buck. 1989. *Toxic Parents: Overcoming Their Hurtful Legacy and Reclaiming Your Life*. New York: Bantam.

Dr. Forward likes case histories and uses them effectively to show how adult children can overcome problems of self—esteem, intimacy or addictions. Dr. Forward is well—known for her work in sexual abuse issues.

Gittleman, Ann Louise, with J. Maxwell Desgrey. 1988. *Beyond Pritikin*. New York: Bantam Books.

The author has taken the Pritikin program, which emphasized a low fat, high carbohydrate diet, and devised a life—style program of her own, correcting some of the problems caused by a low fat regimen. She includes a 21—day diet program plus menu plans, recipes and advice on how to purchase food.

Gussow, Joan, and Paul Thomas. 1986. *The Nutrition Debate: Sorting Out Some Answers*. Palo Alto, CA: Bull Publishing Company.

The authors conduct the "debate" about nutrition by printing and commenting on literature on the subject, an interesting and useful approach; however, the lack of an index makes the book useless as a reference.

Hampshire, Elizabeth. 1988. *Freedom from Food*. Park Ridge, IL: Parkside Publishing Corporation.

This is the story of six people who achieved freedom from their food obsessions. Eating compulsions can encompass any of the following activities: eating for relief, starving occasionally, feeling guilty about amounts eaten, sneaking food, exercising to excess, and many others.

Hancock, Emily. 1989. *The Girl Within*. New York: Dutton.

Probably the major issue for young women with eating disorders is the process of becoming adult. The author interviewed 20 women, predominately white and middle class, and concluded that the key to woman's maturity often lies in reintegrating the androgynous eight— or nine—year—old "girl within" with the woman she has become.

Hatfield, Antoinette, and Peggy Stanton. 1973. *Help! My Child Won't Eat Right: A Guide to Better Nutrition*. Washington, D.C.: Acropolis Books.

Designed to help parents encourage good eating habits in children, the book provides good nutritional information, using clever aids such as cartoons, poems and illustrations to add impact to their message. The authors furnish over 200 menus and recipes. They also give tables of growth standards; weights and measures and conversion values; and a table of food composition.

Hay, Louise L. 1984. *You Can Heal Your Life*. Santa Monica: Hay House.

The author's message explores the mental patterns behind disease and how attitudes affect the course of illness.

Kritzberg, Wayne, 1987. *Gifts for Personal Growth and Recovery*. Pompano Beach, FL: Health Communications.

Each person may have the power of self–healing. This book helps recover the often lost gift. The author lectures and conducts workshops on counseling skills and personal growth, working especially with co–dependents and recovering alcoholics.

Keuger, David W. 1984. *Success and the Fear of Success in Women*. New York: The Free Press.

Not specifically about eating disorders, this is a well–rounded overview of the most common psychological problems faced by the new liberated woman. The author touches on bulimia and anorexia nervosa as well as success phobias, sex identity and much else.

Larsen, Earnest. 1979. *Love Is a Hunger*. Minneapolis: CompCare Publishers.

Drawing on his counseling experience, the author talks about the need for love and the attitudes that build and support it. He advocates theories of Erich Fromm, Rainer Maria Rilke, Rollo May, William Glasser, and others.

Lerner, Harriet Goldhor. 1985. *The Dance of Anger: A Woman's Guide to Changing the Patterns of Intimate Relationships*. New York: Harper & Row.

The author, a psychotherapist at the Menninger Foundation, explores the causes and patterns of anger and provides specific strategies for making lasting change in important relationships.

Listen to the Hunger. 1987. Center City, MN: Hazelden.

The author claims that hunger can signal numerous unsatisfied needs other than the need for food: hunger can mask feelings of anger, fear, loneliness, fatigue and boredom. She makes an effort to help the reader discover, by "listening to the hunger," what the hunger is all about.

Bibliography

Mayer, Jean, and Jeanne P. Goldberg. 1990. *Dr. Jean Mayer's Diet & Nutrition Guide.* New York: St. Martin's Press.

As usual, Dr. Mayer's nutrition advice is down–to–earth and sensible. Goldberg collaborates with Dr. Mayer on his nutrition newspaper column "Food for Thought." In a question–and–answer format, the book debunks food fads and dangerous diets. Weight loss advice is typical of Dr. Mayer's long–held views of health and nutrition: eat a well–balanced, reduced calorie diet and increase physical activity.

McFarland, Barbara, and Tyeis Baker–Baumann. 1988. *Feeding the Empty Heart.* Center City, MN: Hazelden.

This book attempts to explain why children of alcoholics are especially prone to developing the addictive illness of compulsive eating. The authors explain factors in alcoholic homes that may foster eating disorders, including the following: "Alcoholism has progressed far enough that it thwarts the child's ability to develop trust, self–esteem, interpersonal skills, and a solid personal identity. The family uses food to comfort and console . . . The child adopts certain roles within the alcoholic family system."

McFarland, Barbara, and Anne Marie Erb. 1989. *Abstinence in Action: Food Planning for Compulsive Eaters.* Center City, MN: Hazelden.

This workbook attempts to bring needed structure to the compulsive eater's life. It provides worksheets, structured activities and nutritional facts for developing individual food and exercise programs.

Miller, Joy Erlichman, and Marianne Leighton Ripper. 1988. *Following the Yellow Brick Road: The Adult Child's Personal Journey Through OZ.* Deerfield Beach, FL: Health Communications.

Dorothy's journey to Oz in the 1939 movie, *The Wizard of Oz*, is used as an analogy to demonstrate the journey to recovery from compulsive addictions—or from the stress of having been raised in a family in constant turmoil. Illustrations and progression and recovery charts are also used to record the reader's personal journey.

Minirth, Frank, Paul Meier, Robert Hemfelt, and Sharon Sneed. 1990. *Love Hunger: Recovery from Food Addiction.* Nashville: Thomas Nelson.

Using a conversational approach rather than technical language, this book's aim is to explain in layman's terms all about food addiction. It includes a 140–recipe cookbook complete with nutritional guidelines. It also includes 12 reasons for compulsive overeating, questionnaires, surveys, a diet–readiness inventory and exercise and meal plans. The doctors aim their therapy at the whole person, incorporating medical, psychological, spiritual and nutritional needs.

Monte, Tom, with Ilene Pritikin. 1988. *Pritikin: The Man Who Healed America's Heart.* Emmaus, PA: Rodale Press.

This is the complete story of the man who helped popularize the idea of a low cholesterol diet for the treatment of heart disease and over-weight. In addition to Pritikin's biography, the book also provides a succinct overview of the Pritikin program, which in addition to low cholesterol foods, recommends whole grains, fresh vegetables and non-dairy foods.

Mount, James Lambert. 1975. *The Food and Health of Western Man.* New York: John Wiley & Sons.

The author begins with a nutritional history of humankind. In addition to obesity, he deals with infant nutrition, vitamin and mineral deficiencies and diabetes. He also cites health statistics. The appendix contains Sir Robert McCarrison's whole–grain diet, based on a well–known study he did, feeding a "good diet" and a "bad diet" to two groups of rats.

Newman, Mildred, and Bernard Berkowitz, with Jean Owen. 1971. *How to Be Your Own Best Friend: A Conversation with Two Psychoanalysts.* New York: Ballantine Books.

The authors say the following about the book: "We talk . . . about what's awry in our inner world, about frustration and boredom and anxiety, about difficulties with marriage and sex, about the lack of fulfillment in our lives . . . Are we really doing all we can to make our lives more rewarding?" The authors' conversations provide the reader insight into personal issues that may lead to problems of inner conflict.

Oliver–Diaz, Philip, and Patricia A. O'Gorman. 1988. *12 Steps to Self–Parenting for Adult Children of Alcoholics.* Deerfield Beach, FL: Health Communications.

Though written for adult children of alcoholics, the self–parenting process is applicable to all co–dependents, which in this book the authors call compulsive dependents. The authors describe compulsive dependency: "The compulsively dependent self . . . is often control-ling and needing to rescue others, or in turn to be rescued by them. Or due to their compulsive dependency, they will turn to other things in their search for completeness, such as compulsively overeating, compulsive sex, compulsively spending money or working excessively, all in an attempt to be filled up."

Bibliography

Osborne, Philip. 1989. *Parenting for the '90s.* Good Books.

Good parenting is the key to prevention of eating disorders. Osborne introduces four groups of parenting skills: those needed for the "no problem" area, the child's problem area, the parent's problem area and the mutual problem area. This book is intended primarily as a textbook, and the author discusses three popular philosophies of parenting: James Dobson's disciplinarian, Thomas Gordon's parent effectiveness training and B. F. Skinner's behaviorism. Despite its academic focus, however, it is useful for individual parents. Although the publisher normally publishes books about the Amish and the Pennsylvania Dutch, this is not a religious book.

Otis, Arol L., and Roger Goldingay. 1989. *Campus Health Guide.* New York: College Board.

For the potential bulimic, beginning college is a time of special vulnerability. *Campus Health Guide* uses a question–and–answer format and many charts and diagrams. In addition to eating disorders, it covers many topics especially relevant to college students, including the following: environmental health hazards, drug use, sexual health and emotional well–being.

Overeaters Anonymous. 1980. *Overeaters Anonymous.* Torrance, CA: Overeaters Anonymous, Inc.

This is a collection of testimonials by people who have overcome overeating through the OA program. Articles in the appendixes discuss overeating as a disease of the mind, disease of the body and a disease of the spirit.

Overeaters Anonymous. 1985. *Lifeline Sampler.* Torrance, CA: Overeaters Anonymous.

Overeaters Anonymous advocates "abstinent living," which means controlled and careful eating, avoiding foods and situations likely to provoke eating binges. OA stresses mutual support found through meetings and through sponsorship of new members, much like Alcoholics Anonymous.

Pritikin, Nathan, and Patrick M. McGrady Jr. 1979. *The Pritikin Program for Diet and Exercise.* New York: Grosset & Dunlap.

The author originally developed his program as self–treatment for heart disease; he later researched and expanded the program, a combination of diet and exercise, at his Longevity Center in Santa Monica, California. At first controversial, it is now regarded as nutritionally sound except for being too restrictive of fats. The authors include lots of case histories and testimonials. There are also lots of recipes and suggestions for food substitutions.

Pyke, Magnus. 1968. *Food and Society*. London: John Murray.

Interesting insights are offered into humankind's relationship with food, citing religious, cultural and geographic differences in diet as well as the scientific basis for nutrition. The author also describes odd facts and fallacies and the use of food in the magic of primitive societies.

Rodale, Robert. 1972. *Sane Living in a Mad World: A Guide to the Organic Way of Life*. Emmaus, PA: Rodale Press.

This is really a plea to return to more "natural" foods, that is, those that are unprocessed and without additives; however, the author's back–to–the–earth philosophy also advocates sensible eating habits.

Rosellini, Gayle, and Mark Worden. 1985. *Of Course You're Angry*. Center City, MN: Hazelden.

Anger is a normal and healthy emotion; however, chemically dependent people have a special problem with it. A goal of this book is to show readers how to accept and deal with anger without fear and guilt. It contains illustrations, stories, checklists and advice on how to turn anger into a tool for positive growth.

Schaeffer, Brenda. 1987. *Is It Love or Is It Addiction?* Center City, MN: Hazelden.

Love addiction is related to food addiction, like all other addictions. The author helps sort out the unhealthy, addictive elements in relationships and offers ways out.

Shealy, C. Norman. 1977. *90 Days to Self–Health*. New York: The Dial Press.

Dr. Shealy developed an elaborate system of mental exercises that he calls biogenics, which attempt to gain conscious control over the nervous system and thereby, control over life stresses, increasing energy, promoting relaxation and the controlling pain. His dietary advice is middle–of–the–road standard recommendations to eat sensibly; however, when placed within the context of his mental exercise program, sensible eating habits can be developed.

Siegel, Michele, Judith Brisman, and Margot Weinshel. 1988. *Surviving an Eating Disorder: New Perspectives and Strategies for Family and Friends*. New York: Harper & Row.

Bibliography

This book provides practical guidance in recognizing early warning signs of eating disorders, both for oneself or for family members or friends. It gives important advice on how to confront a problem initially and how to seek help. It also offers practical self–help strategies for overcoming disorders.

Smith, Lendon. 1979. *Feed Your Kids Right: Dr. Smith's Program for Your Child's Total Health.* New York: McGraw–Hill Book Company.

As the subtitle suggests, this is a complete children's nutrition guide by a well–known pediatrician. He discusses most of the potential childhood disorders—including obesity—and prescribes their nutritional correctives.

Snyder, Paul. 1980. *Health and Human Nature.* Radnor, PA: Chilton Book Company.

Somewhat erudite, this book nevertheless presents a clear definition of holism and its return to and increasing acceptance by the medical community. Many of the holistic concepts are relevant to weight control and eating disorders because, unlike scientific medicine, holism factors emotions and feelings, beliefs and psychological factors into the healing process, all of which affect eating behavior. The book has chapters dealing with acupuncture, biofeedback and establishing a healthful diet.

Society of Actuaries, Committee on Mortality. 1979. *Build and Blood Pressure Study.* 2 vols. Chicago: Society of Actuaries.

It was from this massive study, first published in 1959 and now updated, that the Metropolitan Life Insurance Company extracted its tables of heights and weights.

Spodnik, Jean Perry, and David P. Cogan, with Julie Houston. 1989. *The 35–Plus Good Health Guide for Women: A Prime of Life Program for Women Over 35.* New York: Harper & Row.

Many women first experience eating disorders as they approach middle age and find that weight gain normally increases with age. The authors have previously published an effective and sensible weight loss diet; here, they describe basic body functions and explain how they may change as women reach mid–life. They emphasize sensible diet and exercise.

Squire, Susan. 1983. *The Slender Balance: Causes and Cures for Bulimia, Anorexia & The Weight–Loss/Weight–Gain Seesaw.* New York: G.P. Putnam's Sons.

Using case studies, the author demonstrates the onset and progression of eating disorders, beginning with childhood and progressing through various social pressures and stresses of work. This is one of the few books on eating disorders to give particular attention to males. It has extensive notes but no index.

Stare, Fredrick, and Elizabeth Whelan. 1978. *Eat OK—Feel OK!* North Quincy, MA: The Christopher House.

Primarily a basic primer of nutrition, the authors also discuss food fads and nutrition myths and give sound advice on planning good eating and nutrition habits.

Stare, Fredrick, and others. 1989. *Balanced Nutrition: Beyond the Cholesterol Scare*. Eastbound, WA: Adams.

This book offers information on obesity, dieting, exercise, and eating disorders, but it is primarily to explain common misconceptions about health and nutrition topics such as cholesterol, flouridation of water, hormone treatments in meat, tropical oils and other health issues publicized by the media. For example, the book debunks the popular idea that cholesterol levels in the body can be significantly altered by diet.

Stoltz, Sandra Gordon. 1983. *The Food Fix: A Recovery Guide for Destructive Eaters*. Englewood Cliffs, NJ: Prentice–Hall.

The Food Fix calls compulsive overeaters "foodaholics," contending, along with most medical professionals, that for some people, food is addictive, much like alcohol and drugs can be. The book seeks to help individuals become responsible for their own health and eating patterns by offering techniques to deal with the emotions involved in destructive eating: depression, anxiety, loneliness, anger and fear.

Stuart, Richard B., and Barbara Jacobsen. 1987. *Weight, Sex, and Marriage: A Delicate Balance*. New York: Norton.

Stuart is the former psychological director of Weight Watchers and at the time of publication, Jacobsen was a doctoral candidate in marriage and family therapy. The authors explore the theory that women's weight problems sometimes provide emotional benefits in a marriage and that some women believe their weight stabilizes their marriage.

Subby, Robert C. 1987. *Lost in the Shuffle: The Co–dependent Reality*. Deerfield Beach, FL: Health Communications.

The author presents insights for the co–dependent who wrongly believes that love, acceptance, security, success and closeness are dependent upon one's ability to "do the right thing." He calls co–dependency a denial or repression of the real self.

Ulene, Art. 1977. *Feeling Fine: A 20–Day Program of Pleasures for a Lifetime of Health.* Los Angeles: J.P. Tarcher.

Self–care and self–caring form the philosophic core of this book by Dr. Ulene, who frequently appeared on NBC's "Today" show with breezy advice about personal well–being. His sections on food and eating emphasize the pleasures of sensible eating as opposed to the pain of dieting.

Vickery, Donald. 1978. *Life Plan for Your Health.* Reading, MA: Addison–Wesley Publishing Company.

The author, a physician, presents a complete guide to good health that not only includes sensible diet and weight management, but includes discussions of drugs, alcohol, accidents, contraception and management of medical needs. The author strongly advocates that the individual, through lifestyle choices, is in charge of his or her own good health rather than the medical professional.

Vincent, L.M. 1979. *Competing with the Sylph: Dancers and the Pursuit of the Ideal Body Form.* Kansas City: Andrews and McMeel.

The author was a professional dancer and is now a doctor. He examines the social obsession with thinness and how it has especially affected professionals such as dancers, models and actors, producing an alarming overrepresentation of eating disorders among women in those professions.

Wassmer, Arthur. 1989. *Recovering Together: How to Help an Alcoholic Without Hurting Yourself.* New York: St. Martin's Press.

Substitute "food addict" in the title for alcoholic and take the author's advice on dealing with anyone with an addictive disorder. He writes from personal experience about co–dependency and uses personal stories to illustrate the devastation wrought by addiction to lives of both addict and co–dependent. He provides guidelines for evaluating organizations that offer help to addicts and their families.

Wegscheider–Cruse, Sharon. 1985. *Choicemaking: For Co–dependents, Adult Children and Spirituality Seekers.* Deerfield Beach, FL: Health Communications.

The author shows how to know the difference between "freedom from" and "freedom to," essential in recovering from co–dependence and addictive relationships.

———. 1987. *Learning to Love Yourself: Finding Your Self–Worth*. Rapid City, SD: Health Communications.

The author offers the following as observable signs of low self–worth: eating disorders; trouble with relationships; physical problems; drug and alcohol misuse; workaholism and frenetic activity; smoking; over-spending; and dependency on "other" people (co–dependence). The author discusses each of these, offering practical strategies along with inspiration for achieving self–worth.

———. 1989. *The Miracle of Recovery*. Deerfield Beach, FL: Health Communications.

This book provides practicle guidance for recovery from co–dependency and addictions. The author, a leading figure in the treatment field of co–dependency and adult children of alcoholics, offers her own story as inspiration.

Weight Watchers. 1985. *Weight Watchers Quick and Easy Menu Cookbook*. New York: New American Library.

For those already in control of their eating, this cookbook is designed to accompany the Weight Watchers diet program. Recipes are divided by monthly sections—many call for Weight Watchers convenience foods.

Whitfield, Charles L. 1987. *Healing the Child Within*. Deerfield Beach, FL: Health Communications.

The author says, "The 'child within' refers to that part of each of us which is ultimately alive, energetic, creative and fulfilled; it is our real self—who we truly are." He describes the journey of discovery in dealing with fears, confusion and unhappiness. His concept of the adult children of troubled or dysfunctional families is generalized rather than focused only on alcoholic families.

Wilson, C. Philip, ed., with Charles C. Hogan and Ira L. Mintz. 1985. *Fear of Being Fat: The Treatment of Anorexia Nervosa and Bulimia*. Revised edition. New York: Jason Aronson.

This is a collection of somewhat technical papers on the development and treatment of eating disorders. The authors use case histories and include some discussion of eating disorders in males. It has extensive notes.

Woititz, Janet G. *Struggle for Intimacy*. 1985. Deerfield Beach, FL: Health Communications.

The author asserts that all who have grown up with addictive disorders or dysfunction in the home must overcome all the learned survival skills acquired growing up in a dysfunctional atmosphere in order to achieve intimacy in relationships.

Woodman, Marion. *The Owl Was a Baker's Daughter*. 1980. Toronto: Inner City Books.

The publisher specializes in books on psychology, using therapeutic approaches of Carl Jung. This intriguing little book is the Jungian view of eating disorders, presented through case studies.

Zales, Michael, ed. 1982. *Eating, Sleeping, and Sexuality: The Treatment of Disorders in Basic Life Functions*. New York: Brunner/Mazel.

This is a collection of scientific papers, including works on physiology and psychology of hunger and satiety, anorexia nervosa and obesity, as well as the surgical treatment of obesity.

PERIODICALS

Blake, Patricia. 1987. "The 'Weight Shrinks' Dig in: Help for Serious or Just Trendy Eating Problems." *Time* January 12, 1987:64.

Bond, William S. 1988. "The Treatment of Eating Disorders." *American Druggist* May 1988:112.

Brice, G. 1981. "Compulsive Overeating: A Personality Profile." *The Australian Journal of Clinical Hypnotherapy* 2(1):1–13.

The number of compulsive eaters is found to be almost epidemic.

Bruch, Hilde. 1971. "Family Transaction and Eating Disorders." *Comprehensive Psychiatry* 12:238–248.

Patterns developed early in life determine the accuracy of hunger perception as a distinct and identifiable sensation. Distortions in this pattern development lead to eating disorders.

———. 1981. "Development Considerations of Anorexia Nervosa and Obesity." *Canadian Journal of Psychiatry* 26:212–217.

Dunn, P. and P. Ondercin. 1981. "Personality Variables Related to Compulsive Eating in College Women." *Journal of Clinical Psychology* 17:43–49.

Food bingeing may be similar to addictive behavior and a way of escaping intolerable feelings. Feelings of hopeless abandonment (during bingeing) may alternate with strict over–control (perfectionism) during starvation phase.

Elkind, David. 1988. "Eating Disorders." *Parent's Magazine* April 1988:190.

Farley, Dixie. 1986. "Eating Disorders: When Thinness Becomes an Obsession." *FDA Consumer* 20 (May 1986):20.

This article is an overview of eating disorders, giving tips for parents and listing help organizations.

Hornaday, Ann. 1986. "The Body in the Mind's Eye and Other News about Looks." *Ms* November 1986:90.

Kiemle, G., P. D. Slade, and M. E. Dewey. 1987. "Factors Associated with Abnormal Eating Attitudes and Behaviors: Screening Individuals at Risk of Developing an Eating Disorder." *The International Journal of Eating Disorders* November 1987:713.

The authors have developed a screening profile to identify potential victims of eating disorders.

Laessle, R. C., U. Schweiger, U. Daute–Herold, M. Schweiger, M. M. Fichter, and K. M. Pirke. 1988. "Nutritional Knowledge in Patients with Eating Disorders." *The International Journal of Eating Disorders* January 1988:63.

Lehrman, Karen. 1987. "Anorexia and Bulimia: Causes and Cures." *Consumer's Research Magazine* September 1987:29.

Nelson, Miriam, and William Evans. 1988. "Nutrition Education for Elite Female Runners." *Physician & Sportsmedicine* February 1988:124.

Peterson, Robin T. 1987. "Bulimia and Anorexia in an Advertising Context." *Journal of Business Ethics* August 1987:495.

To discover the role of advertising in development of eating disorders, this study measured self–image and ideal self–image and related them to the incidence of eating disorders. The authors make recommendations to the advertising industry.

Stoltz, S. 1985. "Beware of Boundary Issues." *Transactional Analysis Journal* 15:37–41.

Foodaholics have pathological relationships, preoccupation with eating and distorted body image.

Strauss, J., and R. M. Ryan. 1988. "Cognitive Dysfunction in Eating Disorders." *The International Journal of Eating Disorders* January 1988:19.

Telch, C., W. Agras, and E. Rossiter. 1988. "Binge Eating Increases with Increasing Adiposity." *International Journal of Eating Disorders* 7:115–119.

It was found that binge eating is more prevalent as the degree of obesity increases.

Van Gelder, Lindsy. 1987. "Dependencies of Independent Women." *Ms* February 1987:36.

Van Strien, T., and G. Bergers. 1988. "Overeating and Sex–Role Orientation in Women." *International Journal of Eating Disorders* 7:89–99.

Wardle, J. 1987. "Compulsive Eating and Dietary Restraint." *British Journal of Clinical Psychology* 26:47–55.

This paper describes binge eating, compulsive eating, and abnormalities of satiety and hunger. The psychological effects of self–denial combined with the physiological effects of food deprivation produce appetite and behavior disturbances.

Wardle, Jane, and Sally Beales. 1988. "Control and Loss of Control Over Eating: An Experimental Investigation." *Journal of Abnormal Psychology* February 1988:35.

Zucker, Preston, et al. 1988. "Eating Disorders in Young Athletes." *Physician & Sportsmedicine* November 1985:88.

FILMS

Eating Disorders: The Slender Trap. 16mm, 21 min. 1986. Van Nuys, CA: AIMS Media.

This film describes all the disorders and gives advice on how to recognize the onset of an eating disorder; also on behavior for avoiding disorders.

The Real Singing, Talking Action Movie about Nutrition. 14 min. 1978.

Junior–high students talk to each other about the impact of food on body development, personality and self–image. Van Nuys, CA: AIMS Media.

The Sugar Film. 28 min. 1980.

This documentary shows how sugar is grown and processed and shows how sugar effects us, both physically and psychologically. Santa Monica, CA: Pyramid.

Superjock. 10 min. 1978.

This film dramatizes the effects of heavy smoking, overweight and improper diet on one's health. An overweight ex–athlete and his son become motivated to change their eating and living habits. Evanston, IL: Journal Films.

APPENDIX

TABLE 1
1983 METROPOLITAN HEIGHT AND WEIGHT TABLES

MEN

Height Feet	Inches	Small Frame	Medium Frame	Large Frame
5	2	128–134	131–141	138–150
5	3	130–136	133–143	140–153
5	4	132–138	135–145	142–156
5	5	134–140	137–148	144–160
5	6	136–142	139–151	146–164
5	7	138–145	142–154	149–168
5	8	140–148	145–157	152–172
5	9	142–151	148–160	155–176
5	10	144–154	151–163	158–180
5	11	146–157	154–166	161–184
6	0	149–160	157–170	164–188
6	1	152–164	160–174	168–192
6	2	155–168	164–178	172–197
6	3	158–172	167–182	176–202
6	4	162–176	171–187	181–207

WOMEN

Height Feet	Inches	Small Frame	Medium Frame	Large Frame
4	10	102–111	109–121	118–131
4	11	103–113	111–123	120–134
5	0	104–115	113–126	122–137
5	1	106–118	115–129	125–140
5	2	108–121	118–132	128–143
5	3	111–124	121–135	131–147
5	4	114–127	124–138	134–151
5	5	117–130	127–141	137–155
5	6	120–133	130–144	140–159
5	7	123–136	133–147	143–163
5	8	126–139	136–150	146–167
5	9	129–142	139–153	149–170
5	10	132–145	142–156	152–173
5	11	135–148	145–159	155–176
6	0	138–151	148–162	158–179

Weights at ages 25–59 based on lowest mortality. Weight in pounds according to frame (in indoor clothing weighing 5 lbs. for men and 3 lbs. for women; shoes with 1" heels).

Source of basic data 1979 Build Study, Society of Actuaries and Association of Life Insurance Medical Directors of America, 1980

Copyright 1983 Metropolitan Life Insurance Company

Courtesy Statistical Bulletin. Metropolitan Life Insurance Company.

TABLE 2
COMPARISON OF 1959 AND 1983 METROPOLITAN HEIGHT AND WEIGHT TABLES

MEN

Weight in Pounds (Without Clothing)

Height (Without Shoes) Feet	Inches	SMALL FRAME 1959	1983	Change Since 1959	Percent Change	MEDIUM FRAME 1959	1983	Change Since 1959	Percent Change	LARGE FRAME 1959	1983	Change Since 1959	Percent Change
5	1	105–113	123–129	18 16	14	111–122	126–136	15 14	11	119–134	133–145	14 11	8
5	2	108–116	125–131	17 15	13	114–126	128–138	14 12	10	122–137	135–148	13 11	8
5	3	111–119	127–133	16 14	12	117–129	130–140	13 11	9	125–141	137–151	12 10	7
5	4	114–122	129–135	15 13	11	120–132	132–143	12 11	8	128–145	139–155	11 10	7
5	5	117–126	131–137	14 11	9	123–136	134–146	11 10	7	131–149	141–159	10 10	7
5	6	121–130	133–140	12 10	8	127–140	137–149	10 9	6	135–154	144–163	9 9	6
5	7	125–134	135–143	10 9	7	131–145	140–152	9 7	5	140–159	147–167	7 8	5
5	8	129–138	137–146	8 8	6	135–149	143–155	8 6	4	144–163	150–171	6 8	5
5	9	133–143	139–149	6 6	4	139–153	146–158	7 5	3	148–167	153–175	5 8	5
5	10	137–147	141–152	4 5	3	143–158	149–161	6 3	2	152–172	156–179	4 7	4
5	11	141–151	144–155	3 4	3	147–163	152–165	5 2	1	157–177	159–183	2 6	3
6	0	145–155	147–159	2 4	3	151–168	155–169	4 1	1	161–182	163–187	2 5	3
6	1	149–160	150–163	1 3	2	155–173	159–173	4 0	0	166–187	167–192	1 5	3
6	2	153–164	153–167	0 3	2	160–178	162–177	2 −1	−1	171–192	171–197	0 5	3
6	3	157–168	157–171	0 3	2	165–183	166–182	1 −1	−1	175–197	176–202	1 5	3

TABLE 2 (cont.)

WOMEN

Weight in Pounds (Without Clothing)

Height (Without Shoes) Feet Inches	SMALL FRAME 1959	1983	Change Since 1959	Percent Change	MEDIUM FRAME 1959	1983	Change Since 1959	Percent Change	LARGE FRAME 1959	1983	Change Since 1959	Percent Change
4 9	90–97	99–108	9	11	94–106	106–118	12	11	102–118	115–128	13	8
4 10	92–100	100–110	8	10	97–109	108–120	11	10	105–121	117–131	12	8
4 11	95–103	101–112	6	9	100–112	110–123	10	10	108–124	119–134	11	8
5 0	98–106	103–115	5	8	103–115	112–126	9	10	111–127	122–137	11	8
5 1	101–109	105–118	4	8	106–118	115–129	9	9	114–130	125–140	11	8
5 2	104–112	108–121	4	8	109–122	118–132	9	8	117–134	128–144	11	7
5 3	107–115	111–124	4	8	112–126	121–135	9	8	121–138	131–148	10	7
5 4	110–119	114–127	4	7	116–131	124–138	8	7	125–142	134–152	9	7
5 5	114–123	117–130	3	6	120–135	127–141	7	6	129–146	137–156	8	7
5 6	118–127	120–133	2	5	124–139	130–144	6	5	133–150	140–160	7	7
5 7	122–131	123–136	1	4	128–143	133–147	5	4	137–154	143–164	6	6
5 8	126–136	126–139	0	2	132–147	136–150	4	3	141–159	146–167	5	5
5 9	130–140	129–142	−1	1	136–151	139–153	3	2	145–164	149–170	4	4
5 10	134–144	132–145	−2	1	140–155	142–156	2	1	149–169	152–173	3	2

Note: Prepared by Metropolitan Life Insurance Company.

Source of basic data: Build Study, 1979, and Build and Blood Pressure Study, 1959, Society of Actuaries and Association of Life Insurance Medical Directors of America.

Courtesy Statistical Bulletin. Metropolitan Life Insurance Company.

Appendix

TABLE 3

TO MAKE AN APPROXIMATION OF YOUR FRAME SIZE . . .

Extend your arm and bend the forearm upward at a 90 degree angle. Keep fingers straight and turn the inside of your wrist toward your body. If you have a caliper, use it to measure the space between the two prominent bones on either side of your elbow. Without a caliper, place thumb and index finger of your other hand on these two bones. Measure the space between your fingers against a ruler or tape measure. Compare it with these tables that list elbow measurements for medium-framed men and women. Measurements lower than those listed indicate you have a small frame. Higher measurements indicate a large frame.

Height in 1″ heels Men	Elbow Breadth
5′2″–5′3″	2½″–2⅞″
5′4″–5′7″	2⅝″–2⅞″
5′8″–5′11″	2¾″–3″
6′0″–6′3″	2¾″–3⅛″
6′4″	2⅞″–3¼″

Women	
4′10″–4′11″	2¼″–2½″
5′0″–5′3″	2¼″–2½″
5′4″–5′7″	2⅜″–2⅝″
5′8″–5′11″	2⅜″–2⅝″
6′0″	2½″–2¾″

Courtesy Statistical Bulletin. Metropolitan Life Insurance Company.

INDEX

A

AA—*See Alcoholics Anonymous*
Abraham, Suzanne 42, 44
Abundantly Yours (AY) 97, 101
Accomplishment Dynamics
　Company 62
ACLU—*See American Civil Liberties
　Union*
Acquired Immune Deficiency
　Syndrome—*See AIDS*
ACTH (pituitary hormone) 55
Actuarial 91
Addiction 91
Adenosine triphosphatase (ATPase) 69
Adipose cells 13, 91
Adipoteinin 53
Adispin 73
Advertising
　newspaper 21
Aging
　weight gain and 9–10
AIDS (acquired immune deficiency
　syndrome) 4
Alcoholics Anonymous (AA) 25, 97,
　104
AMA—*See American Medical
　Association*
AMA Journal 70
Amenorrhea—*See Menstruation,
　cessation of*
American Anorexia/Bulimia
　Association (AABA) (formerly
　American Anorexia Nervosa
　Association) 39, 84, 97, 101
American Chemical Society 61
American Civil Liberties Union
　(ACLU) 65

American College of Physicians
　56–57
American College of Surgeons 55
American Dietetic Association 70
American Heart Association 66
*American Hospital Association Guide to
　the Health Care Field* 107
American Medical Association
　(AMA) 59
American Psychiatric Association 41
American Psychological Association
　65
Americans for Democratic Action
　(ADA) 64
American Society of Bariatric
　Physicians (ASBP) 101–102
American Society of Clinical
　Nutrition 83
American Therapeutic Society 57
Amphetamines 27, 57–58, 60–61,
　66–68, 70, 91
Amphetamine sulphate 55
Andres, Reubin 7–8, 72
Angina 91
Anorexia nervosa 3, 29, 63, 69,
　71–72, 91, 97
　body image and 32
　borderline cases 38
　bulimia and 39–40
　causes 31–33
　counseling 38
　death from 39
　definition 29
　diagnosis 29–31
　early warning signs 35
　in males 47–48
　need for approval 35
　onset 33

prevalence 31
social aspects 34–35
treatment 36–39
  family therapy 37
  forced feeding 36
  group therapy and support
    groups 39, 82, 84, 97, 101–102
  hospitalization 36–37
  outcomes 39
  psychodrama 37
  residential facilities 37–38
  self-help 38
Anorexia Nervosa: Finding the Lifeline
  (book by Patricia Stein and
  Barbara Unell) 36
Anorexia Nervosa Aid Society of
  Rhode Island 82
Anorexia Nervosa and Related
  Eating Disorders (ANRED) 102
Anthropology 91
Antidepressant drugs 72
Antkowiak, John 76–78
Antkowiak, Lara 76–78
Anushka Institute (New York City) 28
Anxiety 91
Appliances
  weight loss 27–28
Arcuni, Orestes 31–32, 34–35, 81
Arenson, Gloria 81
Arnold, Charles B. 7
Arrhythmia 91
Arteriosclerosis 91
Atkins, Robert C. 60
Atkins diet 59
ATPase—*See Adenosine triphosphatase*
Atrens, Dale 81
Avedon, L. 62
Axel, E. 60–61

B

Bailey, Pearl 61
Barbiturates 57

Bariatric medicine 91, 101–102
Basic training, military 15–16
Basil metabolism 91
Baslee Products Corporation 60
Baumiller, Marlene 65
Beautiful People's Diet Book, The (L.
  Avedon and J. Moli) 62
Beauty
  shifting standards of 17–18
Behavior modification 92
  as anorexia nervosa treatment 38
  as obesity treatment 21
"Belt test" 8
Benzocaine 67
Best Little Girl in the World, The
  (book by Steven Levenkron) 37
Better Business Bureau 53–54, 59
Beverly Hills Diet, The (book) 27, 70
Biamine 73
Binge eating behavior 41–42, 92
Bio-Tech Laboratories 70
Blackburn, George 66, 72
Blue Cross 20, 55, 76
Blum, Sam 31
Blumenthal, H. T. 57
Bockar, Joyce
Body Beautiful Inc. 64
Borderline syndrome 92
Bornheimer, J. 61
Boskind-White, Marlene 40
Botticelli, Sandro 17
Boutureira, J. M. 56
Bradwell, D. 60–61
Brewster Produce 63
Brody, Jane 81
Brooklyn College (New York City) 62
Brown, C. D. 57
Brownell, Kelly 4
Brown University (Providence,
  Rhode Island) 52
Bruch, Hilde 30–33, 53, 81
Buddha 18
Bulimarexia 29, 40, 92

Index

Bulimia 3–4, 39–40, 71–72, 92
    alcohol abuse and 41
    anorexia nervosa and 39–40
    causes 43
    definition 40–41
    diagnosis 41–43
    drug abuse and 41
    future trends 48–49
    in males 47–48
    physical aspects 44–45
    prevalence 43
    social aspects 45–46
    treatment 46, 86
    weight fluctuations and 41
Bulimia: The Binge-Purge Compulsion
    (book by Janice M. Cauwels) 40,
    46–47
Bulimia Association of America 86
Butler, N. 59
Buxom Belles International (BBI)
    97, 102
Buzzi, Ruth 61
Bypass surgery—*See Intestinal bypass
    surgery*
Byron, George Gordon 82

C

Cal-Count 68
Caloric intake
    fad diets and 26
Calorie Control Council 73
Calories Anonymous 53
Calories Don't Count (book by
    Herman Taller) 27, 56, 79
Cambridge Diet 27
Carapella, Raymond 63
Carbohydrate 92
Cardiovascular 92
Cardner, Lizabeth 103
Carpenter, Karen 45, 82
Caruso Products Distributing
    Corporation 64

Cassella, Robert 65
Cathartic 92
Cautela, Joseph 58
Cauwels, Janice M. 40, 46–47
Cellulite 27–28, 55
Centers for Disease Control (CDC)
    27, 65, 73, 97
Charts, height and weight—*See
    Height and weight charts*
Children
    obesity in 10
Children's Hospital of Philadelphia 37
Cholecytokinin 73
Cholesterol 69
Cincinnati, University of—*See Clinic
    for Eating Disorders*
Cirrhosis 92
Clark, R. Lee 64
Clearinghouse on Health Indexes 99
Clinical Nutrition, American
    Society of—*See American Society of
    Clinical Nutrition*
Clinical Nutrition Research Units
    100
Clinic for Eating Disorders (of
    University of Cincinnati) 87
Coco, James 22
Codependency 22–23, 30, 92
Community Health Services (CHS)
    97, 99
Compulsion 92
Compulsive eating 92
Congress, U.S. 53, 66, 74
Consumer fraud issues 78–79
Consumer Research (magazine) 43
Cornell University (Ithaca, New
    York) 71
Cortisone 72
Cosmetic surgery 92
    liposuction 23
"Covert conditioning" 58
Cove Vitamins and Pharmaceuticals
    56, 79

Index

Craighead, Linda 70
Crowley, Kerry 18
Curtin, Judge 78
Cushing's disease 56
Cyclic-AMP 61

D

Dallas Morning News (newspaper) 21
David McKay Company 60
De Garmo, Denise 45, 83
Dehydration 92
Dehydroepiandrosterone (DHA) 56
Demographics 92
Densimeter 8, 93
Depression 93
    bulimia and 41
    eating disorders and 44
"Desirable weight"—*See Ideal weight*
Devereaux Foundation 77–78
Dextroamphetamine 61
DHEA (hormone) 27
Diabetes 48, 93
    obesity and 13, 95
Diagnostic and Statistical Manual of Mental Disorders 29–30, 41
Diary of a Food Addict (book by Herbert Greene and Caroly Jones) 83
Diekhaus, Grace 68
Diet Revolution (book) 27
Diets & Dieting—*See also specific diet*
    anorexia nervosa and 35
    as cause of obesity 13
    drugs, injectable 60–61
    pills 59–61
    self-imposed 26–28
Dietz, William 72
Digitalis 57–58
Dinitro-ortho-creso 52
Disability issues 76–78
Diuretics 93
    bulimia and 40, 43

Dobbs, E. C. 52
Dr. Atkins' Diet Revolution (book) 60
Doctors—*See organization, personal names*
Don't Diet (book by Dale Atrens) 81
Dorset Foods 53
Dragstedt, L. R. 52
"Drinking Man's Diet" 59
Drug Guild Distributors 62
Drug Research Corp. 79
Dublin, Louis I. 82
Duke University (Durham, North Carolina) 22
Durham (N.C.) 22

E

Eating disorders—*See also specific type of disorder*
    history and treatment of 3–4, 93
Eating Disorders: The Facts (book by Suzanne Abraham and Derek Llewellyn-Jones) 42, 44
Eckert, Elke D. 47
Edema 93
    anorexia nervosa and 30–31
Education for the Handicapped Act (EHA) 77–78
Elaine Powers Figure Salons Inc. 69
"Elbow measure" 7
Electrolytes 93
    bulimia and 45
    imbalance of 39
Elliott, Cass 82
Emaciation 93
Emetine 93
Emmett, Steven Wiley 82
Endogenous obesity 51, 54
Energy 93
    fat as stored 6
England, obese infants in 12
Enrico Caruso Pure Corn Oil 64
Epidermis 93

Index

"Escape-avoidance" 58
Eskimos 10–11
Estes, Pam 32
Exogenous obesity 51

F

Fabrey, William J. 82, 103
Fad diets 26–28
Fallon, Patricia 82
Family Health (magazine) 64
Family sculpting 22
Farley Jr., John E. 65
Fashion
    obesity and 19
Fat, body 6, 93
Fat Is a Feminist Issue (book by Susie
    Orbach) 85
Fat Liberation Front 66
"Fat Magnets" diet pills 73
Fat-mobilizing substance (FMS) 61
Fatties Anonymous 53
FDA—*See Food and Drug
    Administration*
Federal Office on Consumer Affairs
    60
Federal Rehabilitation Act 75
Federal Trade Commission (FTC)
    54, 60, 63–64, 66
Fee, Ingrid 76
Feeding tube 93
Feinstein, Alvan 56–57
Feldman, William 72
Fernstrom, John D. 69
Fiber 93
Fisher, Hans 103
FMS—*See Fat-mobilizing substance*
Food, Fat and Feminism (NOW
    symposium) 68
Food and Drug Administration
    (FDA) 27, 54, 59–60, 63–68,
    70–71, 97, 99

Food and Nutrition Board (of
    National Academy of Sciences) 69
Food/2 (magazine) 70
Foran, W. 61
Forety, John 4
Formula diets 74
Four Winds (Katonah, New York
    treatment facility) 37
Frazen, R. 52
Fried, G. H. 62
Fried, Jack 63
Friedrich, William N. 82–83
FTC—*See Federal Trade Commission*

G

Garfinkel, Paul 35
Garren-Edwards Gastric Bubble 27
Gastroplasty 23, 70
Geifer, Eldred 67
Genetics 93
Glamour (magazine) 10, 34
Glucose 13–14, 93
Golden Cage, The (book by Hilde
    Bruch) 30, 33, 81–82
Gortmaker, Steven 72
Gout 93
Greeks, ancient 17
Greenberg, Joseph 68
Greene, Herbert 83
Gregory, Dick 83
Gull, Sir William 29, 34, 51, 83
Gundy, Feridun 66

H

Half Personnel Agency, R. 57
Hannon, Bruce 66
Hanscom, Daniel H. 64
Harms, H. P. 52
Hart, Philip A. 56–57
Hartz, Arthur 67
Harvard Medical School Health Letter 35

Harvard University School of Public Health (Boston, Massachusetts) 8, 56
Hauser, Gayelord 83
HCG (human chorionic gonadotropin) 63
Health and Nutrition Examination Survey 10
Health and weight surveys 9
Health Information Clearing House 99
Health spas 24, 60
Heart arrhythmias 39
Heart attacks 93
Height and weight charts 6–8, 30, 54–55, 70, 72, 76, 82
Heinz Company, H. J. 66
Herzog, David B. 46
Hibernation 13, 94
Hirsch, Jules 12–13, 57, 62, 72, 83
Hoffman-La Roche 60
Hohenwarter, Mark 73
Hollander, Anne 17
Homemaker Health Aid Services 68
Hope, Bob 61
Hormone 95
Horne, Marilyn 22
Hot Pants (inflatable shorts) 58
Hudson, Walter 83
Hunter-gatherers 94
Hydrometer 8, 94
Hyperalimentation 36, 94
Hyperinsulinemia 94
obesity and 13–14
Hypertension 94
Hypnosis 57
Hypothalamus 57, 94
anorexia nervosa and 33
bulimia and 43
Hysteria 94

I

Iannicello, Arline 103
Ideal weight 6–9, 71

Illinois Narcotics Control Division 57
Imperiale, A. 61
India
obesity in 71
Infants
feeding practices 62
obesity in 12
Insomnia 94
Institute for Studies of Destructive Behaviors 84
Insulin 13–14, 65, 94
Insurance issues 76–78
International Association of Eating Disorders Professionals (IAEDP) 102
Intestinal bypass surgery 23, 68, 71
Intravenous Feeding 94
Iowa University Medical College (Iowa City) 56
Ipecac, syrup of 71, 94
Isocal 37–38

J

Jack LaLanne health spas 59, 63
Jejunoileal bypass surgery—*See Intestinal bypass surgery*
Jimerson, David 43–44
Joe Weider's Weight Loss Formula XR-7 63
Joffrey Ballet 58
Jolliffe, Norman 85
Jones, Carolyn 83
Journal of Abnormal Psychology 71
Journal of the American Medical Association 14

K

Kangaroo pump 37, 84, 94
Kastor, Hilton, Chesley, Clifford and Atherton (ad agency) 79

Index

Kate's Secret (TV movie) 45, 83
Kellogg Company 66
Kelly Ketting Furth 64
Kempner, Walter 22, 83–84
Kennedy, Donald 65–66
Keys, Ancel 84
Klauka, Joan 102
Klein, Shirley 102
Knapp, Thomas R. 71
Knickerbocker Hospital (New York City) 53
Knittle, J. 57, 62
Koch, Ed 69
Kroger, W. S. 53

L

Lacey, F. B. 60
LaLanne, Jack 59
Lancet (journal) 68
Lankenau Hospital (Philadelphia) 57
Lanpar Company 57
Lanugo 30, 94
Lasegue, Charles 51, 84
Last Best Diet Book, The (Joyce Bockar) 81
Last Chance Diet, The (book by Robert Linn) 66
Laurence, W. L. 55
Laxatives 94
    bulimia and 40, 42–43
Lean Line (LL) 97, 103
Legal issues 75–78
    consumer fraud 78–79
    disability 76–78
    discrimination 76
    insurance 76–78
Levamphetamine 61
Levenkron, Steven 37, 84
Liberty Life Insurance Company 62
Linn, Robert 66
Lipocaic hormone 52
Liposuction 23, 70, 94, 96

Liquid protein diets 27, 65–67
Llewellyn-Jones, Derek 42, 44
Lohman, Timothy 66
Longevity
    ideal weight and 6
Louis, Joe 52
"Low calorie" label 67
Low-carbohydrate diets 26, 51
Lowenkopf, Eugene 69
Loyola University—*See Stritch School of Medicine*
Lynander, Linda 39
Lynch, V. 60

M

"Magic 36" 8
Maisonet, G. 60
Mama Cass—*See Elliott, Cass*
Mandell, Arnold 64
Mannix, Jeffrey 84
Mannix Clinic for Behavior Training and Control 84
Mannix Method, The (book by Jeffrey Mannix) 84
Manz, Esther S. 104
Marano, Joseph 64
Marvex 60
Mason, I. 60
Massachusetts General Hospital (Boston) 71
Massachusetts Institute of Technology (Cambridge) 69
Mayer, Jean 8, 57, 59, 62, 79, 84
Mayo Clinic (Rochester, Minnesota) 82
Mayo diet 59
McCarty, Tennie 30, 45–46
McDermott, Catherine 76
McIntire, Ralph 104
McLaren-Hume, Mavis 54
MEDLARS (Medical Literature Analysis and Retrieval System) 97, 100

Mendelson, M. 55
Menstruation 94
  cessation of (amenorrhea) 91
    anorexia nervosa and 31–33,
    35
  bulimia and 45
Merck Sharp & Dohme 73
Mer-29 (drug) 56
Merker, James F. 101
Metabolism 94
  obesity and 12, 57–58
Methamphetamine 61
Metracal 27
Metropolitan Life Insurance
  Company 7, 30, 53–55, 70, 72, 82
Michigan, University of (Ann Arbor)
  73
"Midtown Manhattan Study' 54
Miller, Estelle 84, 101
Miller, O. N. 60
Millman, H. 53
Millman, Marcia 19–20, 85
Mittleman, Frederick 36
Moli, J. 62
Monster Within, The (book by
  Cynthia Roland) 86
Morton, Richard 51
Mt. Sinai Hospital (New York City)
  55, 76
Mussolini, Benito 52

N

NAAFA—*See National Association to
  Aid Fat Americans*
Naloxone 69
Narcotics and Dangerous Drugs,
  Bureau of 58, 60–61
National Anorexic Aid Society
  (NAAS) 103
National Association of Anorexia
  Nervosa and Associated Disorders
  (ANAD) 103

National Association to Aid Fat
  Americans (NAAFA) 24, 28, 56,
  82, 97, 103–104
National Center for Health
  Statistics (NCHS) 10, 66, 97
National Health Planning
  Information Center (NHPIC) 97,
  99
National Institute of Mental Health
  44
National Institutes of Health (NIH)
  83, 97, 100
National Library of Medicine 100
National Organization for Women
  (NOW) 68
National Research Council 58
NCHS—*See National Center for
  Health Statistics*
Nelson, Gaylord 59
Never Say Diet (book by Richard
  Simmons) 86
New Drug Institute 78–79
New England Journal of Medicine
  12–13
New Spirit (Houston area speakers'
  bureau) 107
New York City Traffic Department
  56
New York Hospital—*See Payne
  Whitney Clinic*
New York Human Rights Law 76
New York State Education
  Department 77–78
New York Times, The (newspaper) 7,
  17–18, 21, 27–28, 31–32, 39, 74, 81
Nicotinic acid 60
Nidetch, Jean 55, 61, 85, 104
NIH—*See National Institutes of Health*
Norcross, John W. 67
NOW—*See National Organization
  for Women*
Nu-Dimensions 59
Nutrition 9, 95

Index

O

OA—*See Overeaters Anonymous*
Obesity 4–5, 95—*See also specific
  types and treatments of obesity*
  causes 11–16, 72
    decreased physical activity
      15–16
    genetic factors 11–14
    psychological factors 14–15
  definition 6
  as disorder 4, 16–17
  inactivity and 15–16, 95
  medical aspects 16–17
  overweight vs 6, 8–9, 95
  prevalence 9
  social aspects 17–20
    discrimination 19–20
    traditional attitudes 17–19
  statistics 5, 7–8
  treatment 20–28
    camps and spas 23–24
    medical methods 20–23
    self-help 25–28
    support groups 24–25
    surgery 23
  trends for future 28
  weight norm measurement 6–9
Obesity Research Center (of St.
  Luke's-Roosevelt Hospital) (New
  York City) 86
O'Brien, Richard M. 70
O'Neill, Cherry Boone 32–35, 85
On Hysterical Anorexia (paper by
  Charles Lasegue) 84
Oral Roberts University (Tulsa,
  Oklahoma) 65
Orbach, Susie 85
Ostopowitz, Elizabeth 56
Overeaters Anonymous (OA) 18,
  22, 25, 97, 104
Overeating
  obesity and 4, 14

Overweight 6, 8–9, 95
  Glamour survey on 10

P

Parrish, R. E. 62
Patton, Sharon Greene 13, 19, 85
Pavarotti, Luciano 66
Pavlov, Ivan 52
Payne Whitney Clinic (of New York
  Hospital) (New York City) 37
Pedometer 95
Pennsylvania, University of
  (Philadelphia) 37
People (magazine) 45
Pepstep 67
Percy, Charles 66
Perfluoroctyl bromide 65
Perlstein, I. B. 57
Peters, Roberta 61
Pharmaceutical Sciences Journal 65
Phase Method 63
Phelps Memorial Hospital (North
  Tarrytown, New York) 71
Phenmetrazine—*See Preludin*
Phenobarbital 55
Phenylpropanolamine
  hydrochloride (PPA) 54, 67–68, 70
Philadelphia Child Guidance Clinic
  37, 63
PHS—*See Public Health Service, U.S.*
Physicians—*See organization, personal
  names*
Physiology 95
*Phythisiologia: Or, a Treatise of
  Consumptions* (Richard Morton) 51
Pica 48, 95
Pignatelli, Princess—*See Avedon, L.*
Pillsbury Company 64
Pima Indians 12, 72
"Pinch test" 8, 52, 95
Pituitary gland 95
  anorexia nervosa and 33

Polivy, Janet 85
Pondamin 61
Porter & Dietsch Inc. 64
PPA—*See Phenylpropanolamine hydrochloride*
Prader-Willi syndrome 48, 95
Prednisone 57
Preludin (phenmetrazine) 55
Premachandra, B. N. 57
Pritikin, Nathan 85
Pritikin Longevity Center 85
Proctor, Richard 69
Protein 95
Prout, T. E. 59
Psychological 95
Psychological Aspects of Obesity (book edited by Benjamin B. Wolman) 11
Psychology Today (magazine) 47
Puberty 95–96
Public Health Service, U.S. (PHS) 9, 54–55
Pump therapy 71
Purge 95

Q

Quick weight loss diet 27

R

Rader Institutes 28
"Reduced calorie" label 67
Regimen reducing tablets 54, 79
Rehabilitation Act 77
Relax-a-cisor 27
Renfrew Center (Philadelphia, Pa.) 72, 82
Rhode Island Medical Society 65
Rice diet 22, 59, 83–84
Richardson, H. E. 52
Richardson-Merrell Corporation 56
Rigotti, Nancy A. 71

Robertson, J. D. 52
Rockefeller University (New York City) 73
Rodin, Judith 11, 65
Rollslim 62
Root, Maria P. P. 86
Rowland, Cynthia 86
Rubel, J. Bradley 102
Rubens, Peter Paul 17
Rue, Joyce L. 101
Rumination disorder of infancy 48, 95
Russell, Lillian 85
Rynearson, E. H. 53

S

Saccharin 64
Sacred Heart Hospital (Eugene, Oregon) 102
St. Luke's-Roosevelt Hospital (New York City)—*See Obesity Research Center*
Salata, D. R. 62
Sanorex 61
Sarfaraz, Niazi 65
Scarsdale Diet (book by Herman Tarnower) 27, 68
Schachter, Stanley 86
Schizophrenia 95
Science (magazine) 69
Science News (magazine) 46
Sedentary 96
See, Jackie R. 73
Seltzer, Carl 8
Sensible Eating Formula 69
Serotonin 96
  bulimia and 43
Sex
  ideal weight ranges and 8
  obesity and 10
Sexual abuse
  bulimia and 45–46

Index

Shades of Hope treatment center (Buffalo Gap, Texas) 22, 28, 30
Shell, William E. 73
Sherman, Walter 55
Sherwin, Robert 66
Shoplifting 42
Simmons, E. 59
Simmons, Richard 86
Simon & Schuster 56, 79
"60 Minutes" (TV show) 68
Skin
 fat and 6
Skinfold test 8, 52, 96
Skinner, B. F. 52
Skinny Liberation 58
Slimmer Shake 63
Slim-Quick 64
Slim-Safe Bahamian diet 83
Slim-Tabs 33 slenderizing tablets 61, 64
Southampton diet 27
Spas—See Health spas
Sports medicine 8
"Spot-reducing" machines 27
Stanford Research Corporation 61
Staniger, Cora 65
Starch blockers 70
Starvation 84
 metabolic rates and 13
Starving for Attention (book by Cherry Boone O'Neill) 32, 35, 85
Stauffer Labs 54
Stein, Patricia 36
Stoler, Shirley 86
Stop Dieting—Start Living! (book by Sharon Greene Patton) 13, 19, 85
Story of Weight Watchers, The (book by Jean Nidetch) 85
Strang, J. M. 54
Stress 96
 obesity and 69

Stritch School of Medicine (of Loyola University) (Maywood, Illinois) 61
Strole, Lee 54
Strong Memorial Hospital (Rochester, New York) 77
Stuart Frost Inc. 64
Stunkard, Albert 14, 54, 70, 86
Stunko, Ronald T. 73
Subby, Robert C. 86
Such a Pretty Face (book by Marcia Millman) 19–20, 85
Suction lipectomy—See Liposuction
Suicide 39, 45
Suicide Prevention Center 84
Syndrome 96

T

Taller, Herman 56, 79
Tarnower, Herman 68
Taufaahau Tupou IV, King (Tonga) 18
Television 72
Temperature
 fat and 6
Tenuate 61
Tepanil 61
Tepperman, J. 59
Thermogenesis 13, 96
Think-Slim weight loss program 58
Thinness
 anorexia nervosa and social pressure for 34–35
Thorndike, Edward 52
Thyroid
 desiccated whole 55
 extract 57
 hormones 58
Timm, Alfred 67
Tonga 18

Tooth decay
  anorexia nervosa and 31
TOPS (Take Off Pounds Sensibly)
  67, 97, 104
Tube feeding 36
Tuberculosis 4
Tufts University (Medford,
  Massachusetts) 8
21st Century Communications 64

U

Undernutrition 70
Unell, Barbara 36
United Airlines 76
Uric acid 96
Utah Medical Association 65

V

Van Itallie, Theodore B. 21–22, 65,
  86–87
Van Prohaska, J. 52
Varicose veins 96
Vincent, L. M. 69
Vitamin 96
Viveiros, Marlene 68
Vomiting
  self-induced 33, 44
Von Noorden, C. 51, 54
Voranil 61

W

Wadden, Thomas 74
Walford, Roy L. 70
Wallace, Mike 68
Weider Distributors Inc. 63
Weight, ideal—*See Ideal weight*
Weight charts—*See Height and
  weight charts*
Weight loss
  camps 23–24

gimmicks 27–28
  hormone treatment as method 27
  and obesity management 5
Weight Watchers (Weight
  Watchers International Inc.) 18,
  24–25, 55–56, 61, 64, 66–67, 69,
  85, 104
Weight Watchers (magazine) 25, 57,
  64
Weindruch, Richard 70
Wells, Linda 28
Western Research Labs 57
Wilkins Center for Eating Disorders
  (Greenwich, Connecticut) 72
Williamson, David 73–74
Wisconsin, Medical College of
  (Milwaukee) 67, 104
Wolfe, Sidney 65
Wolman, Benjamin B. 11
Wolpe, J. 53
Women
  obesity and 18
Woodward, Edward R. 71
Wooley, Susan 87
Wooley, Wayne 87
Wurtman, Judith J. 69
Wurtman, Richard J. 69
Wyden, Ron 74

X

Xerox Corporation 76
X-11 Reducing Plan Tablets 62, 64

Y

Yale University (New Haven,
  Connecticut) 54

Z

Zorek, Jane 55, 76